THE WORK BOOK

What You Do Matters to God

by

Tony Cooke

Tulsa, OK

18 17 16 15   10 9 8 7 6 5 4 3 2 1

The Work Book
ISBN: 978-160683-997-3
Copyright © 2015 by Tony Cooke
Broken Arrow, OK 74014

Published by:
Harrison House Publishers
Tulsa, OK 74145
www.harrisonhouse.com

What People Are Saying About This Book

I have had the privilege of knowing Tony Cooke for over twenty-five years. For as long as I have known him, Tony has had good insight into the practical issues that Christians face. Tony is a minister to ministers and a teacher to teachers. In his latest book, Tony turns his focus to the issue of work in the life of the believer. He reveals the importance of our work to God, and God's plan for work in our life. I particularly like the section of this book where Tony debunks some myths about "secular work" not being "spiritual work." This book will be helpful to any Christian who wants to understand how our *purpose*, our *work*, and our *ministry* are inseparably interconnected.

Dale R. Doty, Ph.D.
Founder, Christian Family Institute
Tulsa, Oklahoma

In *The Work Book*, leadership development specialist Tony Cooke takes a hard-hitting look at something everyone does but few understand as he reveals the importance and power of our daily work. Using the Bible as a guide, Tony takes us on a journey through our own lives and demonstrates that the things we do, the habits we develop, and the things we avoid have a major impact on us—for good or for bad.

The Work Book carefully studies God's original intention for human partnership in creating and building God's will in the earth. Then, moving through the life of Jesus and the examples of Scripture, Tony leads readers to thoughtfully examine their own work and the impact it is having on their earthly and eternal destinies.

I cannot think of a more important book for today's culture—an exhausted and frantically busy generation who often spend their time avoiding the kind of work that will give meaning to life, and thereby lose the kind of rest that restores our humanity. We need this book!

John Carter,
Senior Pastor of Abundant Life Christian Center
Syracuse, New York

In addition to the preaching that I love doing, I have been in the auto repair business since 1980, both as a mechanic and as a business owner of two thriving and successful shops. I know the kind of diligence and hard work it takes to be successful. I've experienced this hard work and success in my own life, and I've seen the importance of a strong work ethic in coworkers and employees who have worked with me over the years.

The truths Tony Cooke shares in this book provide a refreshing look at how God views work, and how we can please God in our work. I've known Tony for over 30 years, and he has always been an example of integrity, excellence, loyalty, and strength. Tony's work ethic is as strong as anyone's I've ever known; he lives what he teaches!

Roy Coggeshall

Business Owner, Mechanic, and Minister

Tulsa, Oklahoma

"Whether it is our everyday work or the work of the ministry, there are no second-class assignments from God." I really like this quote from Tony's book, and it's probably one I will steal. That is one of the things I really like about Tony's books—the sheer volume of well-thought-out and biblically based material suitable for using in the pulpit or in private study. Tony's 35 years of experience working on church staffs and in ministry leadership positions have given him an outstanding perspective that moves way past "ivory tower theology." With the sharp mind of a theologian and the big heart of a pastor, Tony writes in such a way that will be a great help to many!

R. Alan Clayton

Senior Pastor of the Ark Church

Conroe, Texas

As a financial planner and small business owner since 1990, I have seen the tremendous importance of having integrity and a positive work ethic. This essential subject, expertly explored by Tony Cooke, provides valuable insights regarding the work we do in our life and professions. *The Work Book* offers exceptional lessons in how to perform at a high level of excellence to the glory of our Lord.

Michael P. Mazzei, CFP

President of Tulsa Wealth Advisors

Tulsa, Oklahoma

Life and all its facets include many four-letter words. "Work" is often lumped into society's list of four-letter words that have negative connotations. But God assigns us our "ministry" in various forms and arenas—and it isn't always behind a pulpit! Our greatest area of increase comes from our greatest area of anointing. The Apostle Paul took pride in his mandated office; let's make sure we magnify ours. *The Work Book* is a workbook to godly productivity and worship.

Timothy T. Tregoning, DC, CCRD
Founder and Director of Impact Clinic
Broken Arrow, Oklahoma

To some people, reading Tony's new book might be considered "work." However, you will discover that it is filled with inspiring and thought-provoking words of wisdom. Tony did a tremendous job of highlighting all that God's Word says on the subject of work. Before Adam was given a family, he was given a job—a full-time job stewarding God's garden. Yes, Adam was given an assignment with a purpose. *The Work Book* is filled with scriptures regarding God's perspective on work and the blessings promised to those who are faithful in their individual giftings and assignments. Every page is filled with spiritual insight and understanding that will empower you to be the best you can be in all that you do. I am confident that once you finish this book and apply these truths to your life, you'll be whistling while you work!

Michael and Vicki Bang
Senior Pastors of Faith Family Church
Sioux Falls, South Dakota

It's been said that success does not follow a dream; it follows hard work. In our culture so many speak of "work" as if it were a curse, yet work is found in Genesis chapter one prior to the penalty of sin in chapter three. Work is not simply a *good* idea; it was *God's* idea. It can be a system of exchange, turning your talent into treasure, or simply a means to keep idle hands busy. In *The Work Book*, Tony Cooke makes the clear biblical and sociological case for the importance of work in our everyday lives. This is a must-read!

Jerry R. Weinzierl
Lead Pastor of Grace Christian Church
Sterling, Michigan

I believe this book helps bring a needed revelation about work to the Body of Christ. Many Christians feel that their jobs are just a mundane, carnal necessity and don't realize the spiritual significance in what they do. The gifts, talents, and abilities uniquely placed in us by God are designed to help us meet the needs of others and minister to our world. It is through our works that we glorify God.

Tony, as a brilliant teacher, helps us to see our work from the divine viewpoint. I believe this book will help us find fulfillment and respect for the work we do and inspire us to achieve the admonition found in Ecclesiastes 9:10: "Whatever you do, do well."

Ken Vance
Senior Pastor of Vertical Church
West Haven, Connecticut

Many Christians wonder if work, or works, have any place in the life of the New Testament believer under the Dispensation of Grace. When Jesus said, "It is finished," did that mean that there is nothing else for Christians to do? In his unique way, Tony Cooke settles the questions surrounding the place and role of "work" for today's believer. Through his balanced approach to biblical study, Tony gives us line upon line and precept upon precept so we can understand both *God's* part and *our* part in living a victorious Christian life.

Herbert Bailey, DD
Senior Pastor of Right Direction Church International
Columbia, South Carolina

Readers will want to underline, highlight, and tag the pages of Tony's book—it is the perfect balance of scriptures, quotes, and illustrations. Tony effectively imparts the old-school philosophy of the benefits of hard work coupled with new-school truths. I simply love the practical "get down to brass tacks and elbow grease" doctrine that is applicable to everyone.

In his book, Tony points out that God is a worker; Jesus the carpenter is a worker; and the Holy Spirit continues to work in our lives. In a time when we can over-spiritualize and under-perform, Tony teaches us that God worked before He rested. Good hard work precedes and results in a godly rest. Bravo, Tony! Another homerun!

Diego Mesa
Senior Pastor of Abundant Living Family Church
Rancho Cucamonga, California

Dedication

This book is dedicated with great appreciation to the people who labor with us in making Tony Cooke Ministries possible.

Lisa and I have the utmost appreciation for our administrative assistant, Amanda Goodman. She has served with excellence since the inception of this ministry in 2002.

We are also privileged to have others helping us, such as Darcy Veer, who faithfully oversees media production and distribution; Cullen Swanson, who has skillfully managed our website for many years; Jenny Grisham, who has always done superb work in the area of graphic design; and Marissa McLargin, our talented editor. Steve Olsen has graciously volunteered for our ministry for many years, sending out our monthly e-newsletters. His wife, Denise, was especially instrumental in the early years of TCM, working in product duplication and shipping.

We are also grateful for Troy and Joyce Wormell, Julie Werner, and the great team at Harrison House. We appreciate their outstanding work in book publishing and distribution. Faith Library Publications also continues to be a valuable partner in our work. We're also grateful for the teams that have translated various titles of our books into Russian, German, French, Spanish, and Portuguese.

We are very indebted to our board members, Pastors Mark and Brenda Thomas and Pastor John Carter. Their wisdom and counsel have been a great strength and support to us.

I am ever mindful of the many pastors, Bible school leaders, and missionaries who have graciously allowed us to minister to their members, students, and congregations over the years. You have extended a great privilege to us, allowing us to come alongside and co-laborer with you as you carry out your divinely given responsibilities.

Finally, we dedicate this book to the generous partners and friends of Tony Cooke Ministries. The financial support, prayer support, and love you have shown us over the years has made an incalculable difference.

"Work is indeed the highest form of existence,
the highest manifestation of the Divine glory
in the Father and in His Son.
What is true of God is true of His creature.
Life is movement, is action, and reveals itself in
what it accomplishes."[1]
—Andrew Murray

[1] Taken from *Working for God* by Andrew Murray. Copyright © 1983 by Whitaker House. Use by permission of Whitaker House. www.whitakerhouse.com.

Contents

Foreword

I am so pleased that Tony has chosen to tackle the significance of our work in his new book, *The Work Book*.

Almost daily, my job as a physician gives me incredible opportunities to interact with people in their times of personal challenge and difficulty. Early in my career, I had to make a decision about whether or not to fully integrate my faith into my practice of medicine. I had decided that I wanted to be excellent in what I did and to provide medical care with respect, compassion, honesty, and integrity to those who came to my office. But would I be willing to communicate to my patients that my Christian faith was at the core of all I did and that the love of Jesus had transformed my life and could transform theirs as well? Would I let them know that all healing comes from God and not from human beings?

I truly believe that as followers of Jesus we should be willing to share what we believe. For me, this takes place in the medical realm, but it should also take place in other professions—retail, construction, service industries, professional jobs, athletics, and so forth. If we have fully surrendered our lives to the Lordship of Christ, nothing belongs to us. Everything we are and everything we do should honor and glorify Christ and serve to make Him known. Being sensitive to the leading of the Holy Spirit, caring deeply about those with whom we interact, and determining to serve others like Jesus did will help us be both confident and Christ-like in all we do—in the workplace and beyond.

Traveling internationally to serve those in great need has given me the chance to see the Lord work in many amazing situations. Leading teams of young physicians to remote areas affected by disasters in central Africa, southeast Asia, and Central America has taken us to situations where we had to rely on the Lord for physical protection and safety as we provided medical relief, emotional support, and spiritual care to the victims of earthquakes, typhoons, and military attack. In addition, living with my family for extended periods in West Africa and Central Asia taught us the vital importance of trusting God on a daily basis for wisdom, protection, and guidance as we served those in great need.

Training young physicians is an incredible privilege and a big responsibility. Learning to practice medicine with excellence is demanding and time-consuming and requires a lot of hard work. Unfortunately, the value of hard work and the importance of having a strong work ethic is not often taught or valued in our society today, even in the church. At times, work is viewed as a necessary evil, something we *have* to do, not something we are *called* to do.

Too often the emphasis and focus in life is on personal time and fulfillment, on finding time to relax and have fun, and on friendship and family and hobbies; work seems to interfere with those things. However, if we take a Biblical view of work and see it as a gift from God and a calling for which we are prepared, we will be able to approach it with joy and excitement and be shining lights for God in a world that needs to see Him and know Him!

As you study and pursue a deeper understanding of this subject by reading Tony's book, I pray that your eyes will be enlightened to see the significance of the contribution that your life, your work, and your efforts can have on all those God brings across your path.

Mitchell W. Duininck, MD
President, In His Image, Inc.
Tulsa, Oklahoma

Introduction

Where did you get your first ideas about "work," and how were your attitudes about it formed? In your early years, did the adults in your life portray working as a burden or a privilege? What were your first experiences with work? Were they positive or negative? If you grew up in church, did you ever hear messages about the value of work, or were sermons focused exclusively on "spiritual" matters?

Were "good works" such as serving others, volunteering, and demonstrating kindness encouraged in a wholesome way at your church? Or were you brought up in a grace-less church where you were motivated through guilt, taught that getting into heaven was based on how good you were and how many good works you performed? (Thankfully, salvation is a gift from God that we receive by faith, not something that we earn based on our own merits.)

This book is about *work*, and *works*. When we use these terms in this book, we're referring to what we spend our time, energy, and effort doing. "Work" is often thought of synonymously with one's job, employment, or career. In an broader sense, it is what we do to achieve certain goals and accomplish certain tasks. "Works" is a term that often refers to individual actions that are not necessarily job-related in the typical sense, but are those things we do throughout the course of our life. For example, everyone would understand the statement, "John served others by engaging in many good works." The meaning and usage of "work" and "works" can overlap at times, but the main idea is that we work (apply ourselves, exert energy, and act) to produce certain results and outcomes. In short, work *and* works—whether good or bad—refer to what we do with our lives.

How much of a role has secular society played in forming your view of work? I posed a question via social media, asking people to help me come up with a list of songs about work or employment, and allowed both pro-work and anti-work songs. The results were fascinating! I learned that there are many more negative songs about working and employment than there are positive.

If pop or country music was a part of forming your perspective of work over the years, here are some of the messages you may have heard:

❖ You learned from the Beatles about "working like a dog."[2]

❖ Johnny Paycheck describes one of his supervisors as a "fool" and another as a "regular dog," before declaring, "Take this job and shove it, I ain't working here no more."[3]

❖ In "Working 9 to 5," Dolly Parton complains about barely getting by, being used, not receiving credit for work done, not receiving a deserved promotion, and feeling like the boss "is out to get [her]."[4]

❖ With a first line that starts "I don't want to work," the Todd Rundgren song "Bang the Drum All Day" continues:
"Every day when I get home from work
I feel so frustrated
The boss is a jerk
And I get my sticks and go out to the shed
And I pound on that drum like it was the boss's head."[5]

---

[2] Beatles. "A Hard Day's Night." By John Lennon and Paul McCartney. *A Hard Day's Night.* United Artists, June 1964.
[3] Paycheck, Johnny. "Take This Job and Shove It." By David Allan Coe. *Take This Job and Shove It.* Epic, October 1977.
[4] Parton, Dolly. "9 to 5." *9 to 5 and Odd Jobs.* RCA Nashville, November 1980.
[5] Rundgren, Todd. "Bang the Drum All Day." *The Ever Popular Tortured Artist Effect.* Bearsville, April (US) and July (UK) 1983.

❖ Tennessee Ernie Ford tells the tale of a coal miner in "Sixteen Tons":

"You load sixteen tons, what do you get

Another day older and deeper in debt

Saint Peter don't you call me 'cause I can't go

I owe my soul to the company store."[6]

❖ In "Oney," Johnny Cash sings about a resentful man who's retiring after working at a shop for 29 years. He's looking forward to giving his boss "a right hand full of knuckles" as soon as he's received his gold watch.[7]

❖ In "Quittin' Time," Keith Whitley sings of the time clock, "Lord, I love punchin' out like I hate punchin' in."[8]

❖ Bachman-Turner Overdrive in "Taking Care of Business" sings, "You can get to work by nine / And start your slaving job to get your pay."[9]

❖ In "Nothin' But a Good Time," Poison sings, "I'm always workin' slavin' every day / Gotta get a break from that same ol' same ol'."[10]

❖ "The Big Rock Candy Mountain," a light-hearted old country song, refers to a fantasy-land for hobos "where they hung the jerk that invented work."[11]

---

[6] Ford, Tennessee Ernie. "Sixteen Tons." By Merle Travis. Hollywood: Capitol Studios, September 1955.

[7] Cash, Johnny. "Oney." By Jerry Chestnut. *Any Old Wind That Blows*. Columbia, July 1972.

[8] Whitley, Keith. "Quittin' Time." *L.A. To Miami*. RCA Nashville, October 1985.

[9] Bachman-Turner Overdrive. "Takin' Care of Business." By Randy Bachman. *Bachman–Turner Overdrive II*. Mercury, December 1973.

[10] Poison. "Nothin' But a Good Time." By Bobby Dall, C.C. Deville, Brett Michaels, Rikki Rockett, and Jordi Carretero. *Open Up and Say... Ahh!* Enigma, 1988.

[11] McClintock, Harry. "The Big Rock Candy Mountains." Victor, November 1928.

❖ In "Maggie's Farm," Bob Dylan sings, "It's a shame the way she makes me scrub the floor / I ain't gonna work on Maggie's farm no more."[12]

George Carlin, a comedian and social commentator, once said, "Most people work just hard enough not to get fired and get paid just enough money not to quit."[13] Someone else expressed his aversion to work with the remark, "I love work. I can watch people do it for hours." We may spend one-third of our adult life working. Do we really want to buy into the kind of hyper-negativity and fatalism that has been expressed through pop culture? If we apply the Apostle Paul's admonition to not be conformed to this world to the issue of employment, we are certainly going to view work very differently from the way the world sees it.

While negative songs about work are easy to find, songs with a positive message are almost impossible to find. Interestingly, Disney leads the way. The Seven Dwarfs model the best attitude toward labor with "Whistle While You Work"[14] and "Heigh-Ho, Heigh-Ho, It's Off to Work We Go."[15] In Mary Poppins, Bert and his fellow soot-laden workers who clean chimneys demonstrate through dance and song that they enjoy their work and consider themselves to be very lucky.[16]

One secular song that promotes a positive work ethic is Mick Jagger's "Let's Work." In it, Jagger denounces laziness and an attitude of entitlement:

---

[12] Dylan, Bob. "Maggie's Farm." *Bringing It All Back Home.* Columbia, March 1965.

[13] Carlin, George. *Brain Droppings* (New York, NY: Hachette Books, 1997), 206.

[14] Caselotti, Adriana "Whistle While You Work." By Frank Churchill and Larry Morey. *Snow White and the Seven Dwarves* (soundtrack). Walt Disney, January 1937.

[15] Colvig, Pinto, Billy Gilbert, Otis Harlan, and Scotty Mattraw. "Heigh Ho." By Frank Churchill and Larry Morey. *Snow White and the Seven Dwarves* (soundtrack). Walt Disney, January 1937.

[16] Van Dyke, Dick, and Julie Andrews. "Chim Chim Cher-ee." By Richard M. and Robert B. Sherman. *Mary Poppins* (soundtrack). Walt Disney Productions and Buena Vista, August 1964.

"Let's work, be proud

Stand tall, touch the clouds.... /

Man and woman, be free

Let's work, kill poverty."[17]

I'm sure there are other secular songs that extol the virtues of working hard for an honest day's pay, but there are nowhere near as many positive songs about work as there are negative songs.

While it's interesting to see how society-at-large views work, believers will want to know what the Bible says about our efforts and labors in life—both our everyday work (our employment) and those things we do as acts of kindness and service for others.

Works are a major theme from the very beginning of Scripture to the very end. So predominant is the Bible's teaching on work and works that I almost entitled this book *Workology*. I really believe there is a comprehensive theology of works in God's Word. I write this book hoping that it will cause people to see the value of work and to celebrate our God-given privilege and responsibility for making positive contributions in the lives of others through our work.

In spite of its great importance, "work" is a word that many Christians do not want to hear. Christians love words like "grace," "free gift," and "rest." Those are wonderful words—*biblical words*—and they all have a vital role in our Christian life. But "work" is also biblical, and it also deserves our study so that we can rightly determine the difference between what is beneficial and what is futile.

Many today are focused on and celebrating the grace and unconditional love of God. I, too, celebrate God's overwhelming love, as should

---

[17] Jagger, Mick. "Let's Work." By David A. Stewart and Mick Jagger. *Primitive Cool.* Atlantic, September 1987.

every Christian. However, the grace of God doesn't make our works irrelevant or unimportant. Rather, grace—having saved us—enables us to do works that are beneficial to others and pleasing to God. I'm not talking about us doing works in order to earn salvation—that is an impossibility, because salvation is a gift from God that is received by faith. However, our works should express our salvation and give evidence of it.

Some preachers have rightfully stressed that works do not produce salvation, but they have neglected to also preach the fact that works should proceed from our salvation. God has always taken His work very seriously, as has Jesus. And we have been invited, beckoned even, to work and partner with God (and with one another) for our benefit, for the benefit of others, and for God's own glory. Paul even said that "we are labourers together with God" (1 Corinthians 3:9, *KJV*).

This is not a book about getting saved as much as it's a book about expressing our salvation. This is not a book about partaking of mercy as much as it's a book about showing mercy. This is not a book about receiving blessing as much as it is a book about being a blessing to others.

The people under Nehemiah's leadership rebuilt the walls of Jerusalem in amazingly short time. Scripture says that "the people had a mind to work" (Nehemiah 4:6). Today, many people have a mind to be blessed, a mind to receive from God, a mind to be encouraged, and a mind to feel good about themselves—but how many have a mind to work?

If you stop and think about it, everything—absolutely everything—you enjoy in life is the result of someone's work. Do you enjoy breathing air? It's the result of God's work in creation. The same is true of a beautiful sunset or the sound of waves crashing on the rocks by the ocean. All of that is a result of God's work. If you enjoy the apple that comes from the tree, God made that tree and endowed it with the ability to bear fruit.

Do you enjoy knowing that your sins are forgiven? Do you enjoy being a child of God and having the assurance that you are His prized possession? All of that is the result of Jesus' work on the Cross and the work of the Holy Spirit to apply those redemptive benefits in your life.

What about things made by man? Do you enjoy having a cell phone, a vehicle, a chair to sit in, a sandwich to eat? Someone made all of those things. I hope you're glad to be holding this book right now. After I wrote it, someone else had to proofread it, edit it, do the graphic layout, and print it. Someone else had to deliver it to you. Things don't appear out of nowhere; someone has to make them.

Were it not for the work of people, none of the "man-made" things we enjoy would exist. Additionally, we need to realize that even items made by people have their origin in God. God first created the raw materials, and then man manipulated those raw materials to bring about finished products.

And what about you yourself? Do you enjoy living? *You* are God's workmanship. *You* are God's creation. And your friends? God made them as well. All that is good in creation is the work of His hands.

If we want to hear Jesus say "well done," then we need to make sure we are doing some things well. Our lives matter to God because of His unconditional love for us; now it's time to make our lives significant to others through works of love and kindness.

CHAPTER ONE

The Works of God:
He's Still at It

God worked, and we were created.

He works, and we are transformed.

The works of God express His love, power, and grace.

Because of them we are saved from our past,

sustained in the moment,

and have hope for eternity.

B efore we study *our* works, I think it's important to examine *God's* works. After all, since we are called to be godly, it would be good to see if God's example in this area has any relevance to us. One of the first lessons we learn from the Bible is that God, the Creator of the Universe, is a working and productive Being. After reading about the origin of all things, in the second chapter of Genesis, we read:

GENESIS 2:2–3

2 And on the seventh day God ended His work which He had done, and He rested on the seventh day from all His work which He had done.

3 Then God blessed the seventh day and sanctified it, because in it He rested from all His work which God had created and made.

God's personal ratio of work to rest was six to one; He worked six days and rested on the seventh. Right before God ended His work, He took time to review and assess it all. Genesis 1:31 says, "Then God saw everything that He had made, and indeed it was very good." This may seem elementary, but I want to point out that God views work as a good thing and that the results of what He did were good—as a matter of fact, God's handiwork is described as "very good."

The Book of Psalms specifically refers to creation as the result of God's work. David said, "When I consider Your heavens, the work of Your fingers, the moon and the stars, which You have ordained . . ." (Psalm 8:3). Later, David spoke of creation and said, "The heavens declare the glory of God; and the firmament shows His handiwork" (Psalm 19:1).

God doesn't work randomly and aimlessly; instead, His work reveals His greatness and majesty. His work is an expression of who He is, revealing not only His power but also His precision. Psalm 104:24 says, "O LORD, how manifold are Your works! In wisdom You have made them all. The earth is full of Your possessions." Psalm 102:25 says, "Of old You laid the foundation of the earth, and the heavens are the work of Your hands." Many other great references to the works of God appear throughout the book of Psalms:

- ❖ "I will praise You, O LORD, with my whole heart; I will tell of all Your marvelous works" (9:1).
- ❖ "All His work is done in truth" (33:4).
- ❖ "Many, O LORD my God, are Your wonderful works which You have done" (40:5).

❖ "[All men] shall declare the work of God; for they shall wisely consider His doing" (64:9).

❖ "Say to God, 'How awesome are Your works!' Come and see the works of God; He is awesome in His doing toward the sons of men" (66:3, 5).

❖ "Your wondrous works declare that Your name is near" (75:1).

❖ "I will also meditate on all Your work, and talk of Your deeds" (77:12).

❖ "Among the gods there is none like You, O Lord; Nor are there any works like Your works" (86:8).

❖ "Let Your work appear to Your servants, and Your glory to their children" (90:16).

❖ "For You, LORD, have made me glad through Your work; I will triumph in the works of Your hands" (92:4).

❖ "His work is honorable and glorious, and His righteousness endures forever" (111:3).

❖ "I will praise You, for I am fearfully and wonderfully made; Marvelous are Your works, and that my soul knows very well" (139:14).

❖ "I meditate on all Your works; I muse on the work of Your hands" (143:5).

❖ "The LORD is good to all, and His tender mercies are over all His works" (145:9).

One thing is certain about God—He is active! As Longfellow wrote in 1627, "God is not dead, nor doth he sleep."[18] We could add to his remarks

---

[18] Longfellow, Henry Wadsworth. "Christmas Bells." *Our Young Folks*, 1865.

that God is also not dormant, passive, lazy, or inactive. Because God is eternal and omnipotent, He isn't the least bit tired or fatigued. As a matter of fact, Isaiah 40:28 says, "The everlasting God, the LORD, the Creator of the ends of the earth, neither faints nor is weary." Psalm 121:3–4 says that "the one who watches over you will not slumber. Indeed, he who watches over Israel never slumbers or sleeps" (*NLT*).

As we read through the Bible, we see an undeniably clear fact about God: He works! Another clear truth is that we are to perceive, recognize, and praise God for His works. After the Ten Commandments were given by God to Moses, we read, "Now the tablets were the work of God, and the writing was the writing of God engraved on the tablets" (Exodus 32:16). Moses asked, "What god is there in heaven or on earth who can do anything like Your works and Your mighty deeds?" (Deuteronomy 3:24). He also declared, "He is the Rock, His work is perfect" (Deuteronomy 32:4).

God commissioned Moses to deliver the children of Israel from Egyptian bondage, and all throughout that process, God was working. Joshua 24:31 speaks of the elders who "had known all the works of the LORD which He had done for Israel." Judges 2:10, though, speaks of a later generation "who did not know the LORD nor the work which He had done for Israel."

The Prophets Acknowledged God's Working Nature

Utterances that came through the prophets of the Old Testament reveal a clear picture of God and His works. Where the psalms often emphasize God's work in creation, the prophets tend to emphasize God's work toward and in His people. For example, God spoke through Isaiah, saying the following:

❖ "I will again do a marvelous work among this people, a marvelous work and a wonder" (Isaiah 29:14).

❖ "Your people shall all be righteous; they shall inherit the land forever, the branch of My planting, the work of My hands, that I may be glorified" (Isaiah 60:21).

❖ He also said, "But now, O LORD, You are our Father; we are the clay, and You our potter; and all we are the work of Your hand" (Isaiah 64:8).

Other prophets also acknowledged God and His works: Jeremiah said, "You are great in counsel and mighty in work" (32:19), and, "Come and let us declare in Zion the work of the LORD our God" (51:10). Later, Daniel said, "I thought it good to declare the signs and wonders that the Most High God has worked for me" (4:2), and, "He delivers and rescues, and He works signs and wonders in heaven and on earth" (6:27). Even Habakkuk prophesied, "Look among the nations and watch—Be utterly astounded! For I will work a work in your days which you would not believe, though it were told you" (1:5).

Though not a prophet, per se, Nehemiah was given a great assignment to lead the people of Israel in rebuilding their city's broken walls. The people did the actual physical labor, but there was a divine element in the process. Nehemiah 6:16 says, "When all our enemies heard of it, and all the nations around us saw these things, that they were very disheartened in their own eyes; for they perceived that this work was done by our God." Throughout the Old Testament, we see that God is an energetic, life-giving, and productive God. He worked in creation, and He worked on behalf of His people in the Old Testament. But is God still working today, or has He retired?

New Testament Works of God

God did not change when the New Covenant came into effect; He changes not (Malachi 3:6). So it should come as no surprise to us that God did not retire or cease to labor. He continued working in the New Testament, and He is still working today.

Jesus acknowledged that God was still active and working when He said, "My Father is always working, and so am I" (John 5:17, *NLT*). The *Amplified* version renders this verse, "My Father has worked [even] until now, [He has never ceased working; He is still working] and I, too, must be at [divine] work." Later, when Jesus was illustrating His union with the Father, He said, "Don't you believe that I am in the Father and the Father is in me? The words I speak are not my own, but my Father who lives in me does his work through me" (John 14:10, *NLT*). We know that God worked in the Old Testament and through His Son Jesus in the New Testament. God also worked through the apostles in the Book of Acts.

God's Work in the Book of Acts

After the resurrection and after the Church was empowered, the works of God continue to be a predominant theme:

❖ As Jews in Jerusalem observe believers who had just been filled with the Holy Spirit, they proclaimed, "We hear them speaking in our own tongues the wonderful works of God" (Acts 2:11).

❖ When Paul and Barnabas testified before the church council in Jerusalem, they shared "how many miracles and wonders God had worked through them among the Gentiles" (Acts 15:12).

❖ Later in Acts we read that "God worked unusual miracles by the hands of Paul" (Acts 19:11).

God's mighty work doesn't end in the Book of Acts; rather, it continues throughout the New Testament as believers allow the Holy Spirit to work in and through them.

God's Work in the Epistles

The New Testament epistles continue to expound on the works of God and from these writings, God's works are explained. God is seen continually working in, for, and through His people.

As great as Creation was, the greatest demonstration of God's work— His greatest masterpiece—was seen in the resurrection of the Lord Jesus. In the Book of Ephesians, Paul prayed that believers will be able to deeply perceive and understand the reality of their hope and the riches of what God has given. He also prayed that believers will see "what is the exceeding greatness of His power toward us who believe, according to the working of His mighty power which He worked in Christ when He raised Him from the dead and seated Him at His right hand in the heavenly places" (1:19–20).

Other references to the work of God in the Epistles abound:

- ❖ "The LORD will make a short work upon the earth" (Romans 9:28).

- ❖ "And there are diversities of activities, but it is the same God who works all in all. . . . But one and the same Spirit works all these things, distributing to each one individually as He wills" (1 Corinthians 12:6, 11).

- ❖ "For He who worked effectively in Peter for the apostleship to the circumcised also worked effectively in me toward the Gentiles" (Galatians 2:8).

❖ ". . . according to the purpose of Him who works all things according to the counsel of His will" (Ephesians 1:11).

❖ "For we are His workmanship . . ." (Ephesians 2:10).

❖ "Now to Him who is able to do exceedingly abundantly above all that we ask or think, according to the power that works in us . . ." (Ephesians 3:20).

❖ "He who has begun a good work in you will complete it until the day of Jesus Christ" (Philippians 1:6).

❖ "For it is God who works in you both to will and to do for His good pleasure" (Philippians 2:13).

❖ ". . . buried with Him in baptism, in which you also were raised with Him through faith in the working of God, who raised Him from the dead" (Colossians 2:12).

❖ Hebrews 13:21 says, that the God of peace will "make you complete in every good work to do His will, working in you what is well pleasing in His sight."

We also see in the epistles that God's very Word *also* works. For example, in First Thessalonians 2:13, Paul referred to "the word of God, which also effectively works in you who believe."

God's Works in the Revelation

God's work spans Genesis to Revelation. And in the same way that the psalms praise God for His mighty works, the last book of the Bible shows God being praised for the same thing in heaven. Revelation 15:3 says, "They sing the song of Moses, the servant of God, and the song of the Lamb, saying: 'Great and marvelous are Your works, Lord God Almighty! Just and true are Your ways, O King of the saints!'" In Revelation 1:4, the

Apostle John extends a greeting from God as the One "who is and who was and who is to come." This verse implies that our Triune God is the God who *is* working, who *has* worked, and *is yet* to work. Because God *did* work, we were created and redeemed. Because God *does* work, we are kept and sustained. And because God *will* work, we have a future and a hope.

Job's Life Was Changed by Perceiving God Through His Works

Before we leave this topic of God's works, I want us to go back to what were perhaps the first writings of Scripture, the Book of Job.

Job was a righteous man; God himself testified of that. And yet Job was very limited in his knowledge of God. He went through some terrible situations, suffered catastrophic losses, and was deeply grieved and wounded. In his horrific pain, Job lashed out at God and said many things that were incorrect. Later, after God had revealed Himself to Job, Job confessed, "I will cover my mouth with my hand. I have said too much already. I have nothing more to say" (Job 40:4–5, *NLT*). Job further recanted, "I was talking about things I knew nothing about, things far too wonderful for me. . . . I take back everything I said, and I sit in dust and ashes to show my repentance" (Job 42:3, 6, *NLT*).

Where did Job's new, clearer perceptions of God come from? How did Job come to know God in a way that he never had before? It all started when a young man named Elihu was moved by the Spirit of God to rebuke Job and address some very vital issues. Elihu confronted Job, saying, "Listen to this, O Job; Stand still and consider the wondrous works of God" (Job 37:14). Elihu continued, encouraging Job to consider "those wondrous works of Him who is perfect in knowledge" (Job 37:16). Shortly before this, Elihu admonished Job, "Remember to magnify His work, of which men have sung" (Job 36:24).

Why this emphasis on the works of God? Elihu knew that Job needed to see God's true nature and character. As Elihu's remarks came to an end, God picked up right where Elihu left off, and God challenged Job along the same lines. God wanted Job to come to know Him, and God basically said, "Job, if you want to know Me, look at My works!" Consider some of God's statements to Job:

❖ "Where were you when I laid the foundations of the earth?" (Job 38:4, *NLT*).

❖ "Have you ever commanded the morning to appear and caused the dawn to rise in the east? Have you made daylight spread to the ends of the earth?" (Job 38:12-13, *NLT*).

❖ "Can you direct the movement of the stars .... Can you direct the constellations through the seasons?" (Job 38:31–32, *NLT*).

❖ "Do you know the laws of the universe? Can you use them to regulate the earth?" (Job 38:33, *NLT*).

❖ "Is it your wisdom that makes the hawk soar and spread its wings toward the south?" (Job 39:26, *NLT*).

God's rhetorical questions had a radical impact on Job and changed his life, and they were all referencing God's works—the awesomeness of His creation and His awesome sustaining of the universe.

Why did these statements about God's works change Job's view of God's character? I believe Romans 1:20 has the answer: "For ever since the world was created, people have seen the earth and sky. Through everything God made, they can clearly see his invisible qualities—his eternal power and divine nature" (*NLT*). God's invisible qualities, His eternal power, and divine nature can be seen through all of the things He made—through His works! God revealed Himself to Job through His works. *What God had done* gave Job insight into *Who God is.* This should come as no surprise, because every person's actions say a lot about his or her character. Proverbs 20:11 says, "Even a child is known by his deeds, whether what he does is pure and right."

Later, the people of Israel would learn about God through the Law. Later yet, people would receive a great revelation of God through the person and work of the Lord Jesus Christ. But Job learned about God through His works—through observing not only all that the Creator had made, but also through observing God's sustaining and governance of the natural world.

What God does matters—His works reveal His character and intent. We'll discover later in this book that the same is true for us. Our works—what we do outwardly, and how we do it—speak volumes about what is in our hearts.

Quotes Worth Remembering

"I thank Thee, my Creator and Lord, that Thou hast given me this joy in Thy creation, this delight in the works of Thy hands; I have shown the excellency of Thy works unto man, so far as my finite mind was able to comprehend Thine infinity."
—Johannes Kepler

"Nobody seriously believes the universe was made by God without being persuaded that He takes care of His works."
—John Calvin

"God is the best and most ordered workman of all."
—Copernicus

"The human body has been called the microcosm of the universe, a little world of wonders and a monument of divine wisdom and power, sufficient to convince the most incredulous mind of the existence of the Great Designer."
— A.B. Simpson

Questions for Reflection and Discussion

1. Do you feel like you've taken the time to recognize and appreciate the works of God, or have you tended to take His works for granted?

2. What are some of the works of God that you appreciate most? What has He done that has most influenced you and been the most meaningful?

3. What does knowing that God worked six days and rested on the seventh mean to you?

4. What basis do we have for believing that God continues to work actively today? How does the fact that God is currently working affect us?

5. Job was powerfully moved when he considered the work of God in creation. Today, we can know much more about creation through the telescope and the microscope; we can see awe-inspiring and wonder-producing sites that ancient man could not imagine. And yet, the more mankind advances in his ability to see and know the unseen things of the universe (unseen to the naked eye), the more people are often blinded to God. What are your reflections as you consider God's work in creation?

REFLECTIONS FROM READERS

One very important aspect of God's work is His role as our Father. Since we are created in His image, it stands to reason that one of *our* most important jobs in life, if we become a parent, is to take our role seriously and to parent well.

Joan from South Dakota,
who raised four boys and has twelve grandchildren, writes:

Looking back now, I know that I was not just a mother, but I was also called by God to raise champions. This doesn't apply to just me; I believe motherhood is a high calling and is tremendously important in God's plan.

In the early days, though, I didn't grasp my role in God's plan at all. Instead, motherhood was quite overwhelming and stressful, and I had not really learned anything beneficial from my own upbringing that could help me as I raised my own children. I was very unhappy, but no one knew it.

In spite of my frustrations, I know I did one thing right. On each infant baptism day at church, I promised God to give my four boys back to Him—just like Hannah did with Samuel—if He would only help me raise them. I knew I didn't know how to raise my children, so this was my silent prayer to God alone.

My life changed at a Billy Graham ladies luncheon in Minneapolis. The speaker explained how God had told her to apologize to her grandchildren when she had been too hard on them. I couldn't wait to get home and do the same thing with my four boys. They just looked at me, but I knew I had changed. I had learned something positive to work on—a handle to grab. I made the choice to raise champions to the best of my ability. I had something to do, and with God's help I would be a better mother.

We got plaques with each of the boy's names on them along with a Bible verse, and it is amazing that my sons all turned out to be like the Bible verse on their plaque. They saw themselves that way, and it was a positive influence for them. We demanded respect from them—to each other, to their dad and me, to their teachers, and so forth. We got them involved in positive activities and kept them busy.

I would encourage every woman who becomes a mother to pray and realize the importance of time spent with your children. If you feel inadequate to fulfill the roles you have been assigned, let the scriptures about who you are in Christ encourage you. Say about yourself what God says about you, including, "I can do all things through Christ who strengthens me" (Philippians 4:13).

With God's help, I did all I could to honor His call, even though I didn't even view it as a calling in the early days. Yes, it was hard work, but I have no regrets! I am thankful I had the opportunity to be a stay-at-home mom. I am eighty years old now, and I am blessed, happy, and honored by our children. Three of our sons went into full-time ministry, and Mitch (who wrote the Foreword of this book) became a physician who ministers internationally through his medical practice. I can't imagine a greater joy than to have our children rise up and call me blessed (Proverbs 31:28).

CHAPTER TWO

The Works of Jesus: His Works Reveal the Father

"Divine Fatherhood means that God is all, and gives all, and works
all. Divine Sonship means continual dependence on the Father,
and the reception, moment by moment,
of all the strength needed for His work."[19]
—Andrew Murray

Since God is revealed as a worker throughout Scripture, it should come as no surprise that Jesus is clearly portrayed as a worker as well. After all, Colossians 1:15 says that Jesus "is the exact likeness of the unseen God [the visible representation of the invisible]" (*AMP*). Likewise, Hebrews 1:3 states, "He is the sole expression of the glory of God [the Light-being, the out-raying or radiance of the divine], and He is the perfect imprint and very image of [God's] nature" (*AMP*). Even Jesus said, "He who has seen Me has seen the Father" (John 14:9).

With this in mind, we should expect to see a strong correlation between the way the Father works and the way Jesus works. They are both workers. As a matter of fact, the Father did His work through Jesus.

---

[19] Taken from *Working for God* by Andrew Murray. Copyright © 1983 by Whitaker House. Use by permission of Whitaker House. www.whitakerhouse.com.

JOHN 14:10 (*NLT*)

10 Don't you believe that I am in the Father and the Father is in me? The words I speak are not my own, but my Father who lives in me does his work through me.

Jesus was continually aware of the Father's Presence and the Holy Spirit's anointing (Acts 10:38) working in and through Him. If Jesus worked and yet relied entirely on the ability of God, how much more do we need to trust God's empowerment in whatever we do for the Lord?

When the works of Jesus are mentioned, people typically think of the outstanding healings and miracles He performed, the messages He preached, and the eternally significant redemptive work He carried out in His death, burial, and resurrection. As vital as those are to us, we don't want to overlook an earlier aspect of His work—the work that He did as a carpenter.

In Mark 6:3, the people of Jesus' hometown disparagingly identify Jesus as "just a carpenter," which is undoubtedly a reference to what Jesus did vocationally before entering ministry. Matthew 13:55 points out that Jesus was also referred to as "the carpenter's son." One commentary notes, "A carpenter (τέκτων) was typically a woodworking craftsman who built furniture and utensils, doors and doorframes, and prepared roofing beams; he may at times have doubled as a brick mason."[20] Another commentary explains that the word *carpenter* is "used predominantly of workers in wood, though it can be applied to craftsmen of other sorts, such as masons, sculptors, or smiths. In a small village the τέκτων would need to be versatile,

---

[20] Nolland, John. *The Gospel of Matthew: A Commentary on the Greek Text. New International Greek Testament Commentary* (Grand Rapids, MI; Carlisle: W.B. Eerdmans; Paternoster Press), 2005.

able to deal both with agricultural and other implements and also with the construction and repair of buildings."[21]

The custom in that day was for fathers to train their sons in their own occupation. It stands to reason, then, that Jesus would have worked alongside Joseph in His early days, and perhaps even up to the time that He stepped into ministry around the age of 30 (Luke 3:23).

William Barclay considers why Jesus may have not begun preaching until that age:

> Why did he spend thirty years in Nazareth when he had come to be the saviour of the world? It is commonly said that Joseph died fairly young and that Jesus had to take upon himself the support of Mary and of his younger brothers and sisters, and that not until they were old enough to take the business on their own shoulders, did he feel free to leave Nazareth and go into the wider world.[22]

Whether Barclay's speculation is correct or not, it is apparent from Scripture that Jesus worked as a carpenter prior to entering the ministry. I believe that Jesus would have engaged in His carpentry work for the glory of God the same way He ministered to please and bring glory to His Father. Every bench He made, every door He framed, and every house He built would have all been completed with an excellence that would have honored His Father.

Too often, we grow impatient, waiting for our dream job or the chance to pursue our calling. But when we labor with excellence as unto the Lord, every step of our journey is not only valuable preparation; it's also

---

[21] France, R. T. *The Gospel of Mark: A Commentary on the Greek Text. New International Greek Testament Commentary* (Grand Rapids, MI; Carlisle: W.B. Eerdmans; Paternoster Press), 2002.

[22] Barclay, William, ed. "The Gospel of Luke." *The Daily Study Bible Series* (Philadelphia, PA: The Westminster John Knox Press), 1975.

meaningful in its own right. J. Oswald Sanders noted the same principle about Jesus' work:

> It is a challenging thought, and one that should be closely observed by those who are preparing for a life of service to God, that our divine Lord spent six times as long working at the carpenter's bench as He did in His world-shaking ministry. He did not shrink the hidden years of preparation. Preparatory years are important years. Jesus must be about His Father's business and doing His Father's will. If that will involved eighteen hidden, laborious, tedious years, He would not succumb to fleshly impatience, but would obey with delight.[23]

When we work with the right attitude and for the right purpose, no labor is ever in vain. We would do well to follow Jesus' example as we pursue God's unique plan for our life.

Jesus' Works in Ministry

What Jesus did in ministry was described as work, and yet it was no doubt a labor of love. Because Jesus saw His exertions upon this earth as expressions of the Father's will and power, He did not consider work an option, revealing, "I must work the works of Him who sent Me while it is day; the night is coming when no one can work" (John 9:4). We know that doing God's work brought Jesus great fulfillment because He likened it to physical sustenance, saying, "My food is to do the will of Him who sent Me, and to finish His work" (John 4:34).

Jesus also saw carrying out His assignment as a way to glorify God. Toward the end of His life, Jesus asserted, "I have glorified You on the earth. I have finished the work which You have given Me to do" (John

---

[23] Sanders, J. Oswald. *The Incomparable Christ* (Chicago, Illinois: Moody Publishers, 1952), 34.

17:4). *The Message* version renders this, "I glorified you on earth by completing down to the last detail what you assigned me to do."

Countless Christians have prayed, "God, please help me be more like Jesus!" Did you realize that when people pray that way, they are—among other things—asking God to help them *be a worker*? If we are going to be like Jesus, then we are going to be compelled by the love of God to work for His glory and to work according to His plan and purpose.

Jesus' Works Were Widely Recognized

Toward the end of Jesus' earthly ministry, we read that "the whole multitude of the disciples began to rejoice and praise God with a loud voice for all the mighty works they had seen" (Luke 19:37). This wasn't the first time Jesus' works were acknowledged. In Matthew 11:12 we learn that John the Baptist "had heard in prison about the works of Christ." Jesus' works were known far and wide. Even His enemies acknowledged the significance of His works. In John 11:47 we read, "Then the chief priests and the Pharisees gathered a council and said, 'What shall we do? For this Man works many signs.'" Jesus was known by His deeds.

When Jesus ministered in the area where he had grown up, people asked, "Where did this Man get this wisdom and these mighty works?" (Matthew 13:54). Instead of allowing their faith to be inspired by the anointing of God that was upon Jesus' life, they became offended because they focused on Jesus' earthly connections—His family. We then read that Jesus "did not do many mighty works there because of their unbelief" (Matthew 13:58). In other words, we can say that Jesus worked mightily everywhere *that He could*, but He did not work at His fullest potential where His work was not welcomed.

Jesus' Works Had a Purpose

Jesus lived a fruitful life, and He occupied Himself doing good works that expressed the love of the Father, engaging in deeds that truly blessed humanity. Our Savior's works were designed to reveal the Father and to validate both the identity and the words of the Lord Jesus. Consider these statements Jesus made:

- ❖ "For the Father loves the Son, and . . . He will show Him greater works than these, that you may marvel" (John 5:20).

- ❖ "The works which the Father has given Me to finish—the very works that I do—bear witness of Me, that the Father has sent Me" (John 5:36).

- ❖ "I told you, and you do not believe. The works that I do in My Father's name, they bear witness of Me" (John 10:25).

- ❖ "Many good works I have shown you from My Father. For which of those works do you stone Me?" (John 10:32).

- ❖ "If I do not do the works of My Father, do not believe Me; but if I do, though you do not believe Me, believe the works, that you may know and believe that the Father is in Me, and I in Him" (John 10:37–38).

- ❖ Believe Me that I am in the Father and the Father in Me, or else believe Me for the sake of the works themselves" (John 14:11).

Jesus wanted people to believe in Him based on His words, but for those who wouldn't simply believe He was who He said He was, He also revealed His divine nature through His mighty works.

Earlier in this chapter we looked at John 14:10 where Jesus says, "The Father who dwells in Me does the works." This verse reveals a key to understanding the pattern that God has in mind for all of us. Jesus saw no disconnect between His relationship with God and His work assignment. Thus, He relied entirely upon the Father, yielding to God's power and ability. To Jesus, work was not something that He did independently and separately from the Father, but something that the Father did in and through Him. This is why Jesus didn't consider work a grievous chore or heavy burden, but a delight.

If we grasp Jesus' dependence on the Father and follow His faith, our work and works will be revolutionized. We will move from self-reliance and self-effort to trusting God to infuse and empower our actions. For our works to be all they were meant to be, we must fully receive God's work *for* us, fully yield to God's work *in* us, and fully express God's work *through* us.

We see cause and effect with the works of Jesus: *the cause* was the Father working through Him, and *the effect* was not only the glory of God, but also a testimony and witness to people. Jesus' works were undeniable proofs of God's love and concern for humanity, and yet people—in their blindness and hardness of heart—still found ways to reject Christ and to remain unrepentant. Consider the role of Jesus' works in one of His most stinging rebukes.

MATTHEW 11:20–23

20 Then He began to rebuke the cities in which most of His mighty works had been done, because they did not repent:

21 "Woe to you, Chorazin! Woe to you, Bethsaida! For if the mighty works which were done in you had been done in Tyre and Sidon, they would have repented long ago in sackcloth and ashes.

22 But I say to you, it will be more tolerable for Tyre and Sidon in the day of judgment than for you.

23 And you, Capernaum, who are exalted to heaven, will be brought down to Hades; for if the mighty works which were done in you had been done in Sodom, it would have remained until this day."

Clearly, the works of Jesus were designed to not only express the love of God, but to also challenge men to believe in Jesus and to recognize and receive the divine nature of His mission.

The Great Redemptive Work of Christ

Jesus did so many amazing things while He was here on earth. He revealed the truth and revealed the Father. He healed the sick, performed miracles, and had compassion on the hurting. The Apostle John, at the conclusion of his gospel, said, "There are also many other things that Jesus did, which if they were written one by one, I suppose that even the world itself could not contain the books that would be written" (John 21:25).

Even though Jesus did so many things, there was an ultimate purpose—a prime directive for His coming to this earth. Consider what Jesus said about His reason for being here:

- ❖ "The Son of Man did not come to be served, but to serve, and to give His life a ransom for many" (Matthew 20:28).

- ❖ "God did not send His Son into the world to condemn the world, but that the world through Him might be saved" (John 3:17).

- ❖ "The Son also became flesh and blood. For only as a human being could he die, and only by dying could he break the power of the devil, who had the power of death. Only in this way could he set free all who have lived their lives as slaves to the fear of dying.... Therefore, it was necessary for him to be made in every respect like us, his brothers and sisters, so that he could be our merciful and faithful High Priest before God. Then he could offer a sacrifice that would take away the sins of the people" (Hebrews 2:14-15, 17 *NLT*).

❖ "He was manifested to take away our sins" (1 John 3:5).

❖ As Jesus anticipated His death on the cross, he said, "Now My soul is troubled, and what shall I say? 'Father, save Me from this hour'? But for this purpose I came to this hour" (John 12:27).

Jesus understood that the primary purpose for His coming to earth was to redeem mankind back to God, and this involved His substitutionary death for the sin of mankind. His redemptive work—purchasing mankind back to God—was not an afterthought or incidental; it was the eternal purpose of God. Peter called Jesus' death a "prearranged plan" (Acts 2:23 *NLT*), and Revelation 13:8 calls Jesus "the Lamb slain from the foundation of the world."

Three times in the Book of Hebrews we are reminded that after He endured the cross, offered one sacrifice for mankind forever, and purged our sins, Jesus sat down at the right hand of God (1:3; 10:12; 12:2). This truth—the finished work of Christ—is one of the most powerful and liberating truths we can ever embrace and celebrate. Because of what Jesus did, all who accept God's gracious gift have right-standing with God and a new identity; forgiveness and freedom have been made available to us in full measure!

How Is Jesus Working Today?

However, that aspect of Christ's work—the acquisition of our redemption—does not mean that Jesus is now in retirement, on vacation, or on some kind of leave of absence. Jesus' redemptive suffering as our Savior is completely finished, and yet He is still working on our behalf. We can rightly say that Christ's current work is entirely founded and based upon His finished work.

Jesus has not gone into early retirement. He is active, alive, and doing far more than most can imagine. It is interesting that when Luke made his initial remarks in the Book of Acts (which is a sequel to the Gospel of Luke), he said, "In my first book I told you, Theophilus, about everything Jesus began to do and teach until the day he was taken up to heaven" (Acts 1:1–2, *NLT*). It seems to me that Luke was saying, "In my first book—the Gospel of Luke—I told you about what Jesus began to do until the time He was taken up into heaven. Now I'm going to tell you about what Jesus has continued to do since He ascended into heaven."

1. **Jesus Is Working Today as Our Advocate, Intercessor, and High Priest.**

    Having already encouraged believers not to sin, the Apostle John then said, "But if anyone does sin, we have an advocate who pleads our case before the Father. He is Jesus Christ, the one who is truly righteous" (1 John 2:1, *NLT*). The word "advocate" here is best understood by us today as *a defense attorney*. The "accuser of the brethren" (Revelation 12:10) will no doubt slander and malign God's children, but Jesus defends us and speaks on our behalf.

Other translations describing righteous Jesus as our "advocate" include:

❖ "He speaks on our behalf when we come into the presence of the Father" (*GW*).

❖ "We have someone who pleads with the Father on our behalf" (*GNT*).

❖ "We have one who speaks to the Father for us. He stands up for us" (*NIRV*).

❖ "We have one who speaks to the Father in our defense" (*NIV*).

❖ "We have a Priest-Friend in the presence of the Father" (*MSG*).

Aren't you glad that Jesus is still working on our behalf?

Knowing that He is our advocate brings us the understanding that Jesus is for us, not against us. The Apostle Paul asked a powerful question and then provided an even more powerful answer: "Who then will condemn us? Will Christ Jesus? No, for He is the one who died for us and was raised to life for us and is sitting at the place of highest honor next to God pleading for us" (Romans 8:34, *NLT*). The *New King James Version* translates this as "makes intercession for us." The intercessory work of Jesus on our behalf is grounded in the fact that He is our High Priest.

The Book of Hebrews makes much of Jesus' role as our High Priest. By studying this portion of Scripture, we can discover what Jesus is currently doing for us and every believer.

❖ Hebrews 4:15 says, "This High Priest of ours understands our weaknesses" (*NLT*).

❖ "God qualified him as a perfect High Priest" and "God designated him to be a High Priest in the order of Melchizedek" (Hebrews 5:9–10, *NLT*).

❖ Jesus' priesthood is perpetual because "He lives forever to intercede with God on their behalf" (Hebrews 7:25, *NLT*).

❖ Hebrews 9:24 says, "Christ has entered into heaven itself to appear now before God as our advocate" (*NLT*).

I can't imagine anything more encouraging to a believer! Jesus sits at the right hand of God, and no matter our weakness or infirmity, He is interceding—pleading—on our behalf. When we have sinned, He is our advocate with the Father. What comfort! What security! What assurance![24]

2. Jesus Is Working Today as Our Shepherd.

In one of the most beloved of all the psalms, David spoke timeless words of comfort: "The Lord is my shepherd; I shall not want" (Psalm 23:1). Countless generations of people have drawn strength and consolation from these words, and it is good to know that Jesus is still the Shepherd who leads, guides, and consoles His people. Peter described Jesus, in His current-day ministry, as "the Chief Shepherd" (1 Peter 5:4) and as the "Shepherd and Guardian" of our souls (1 Peter 2:25, *NLT*).

3. Jesus Is Working Today as the Head of the Church.

The Body of Christ is not without a Commander in Chief. Paul said that Jesus "is the head of the body, the church" (Colossians 1:18). *The Message* renders this verse, "When it comes to the church, [Jesus] organizes and holds it together, like a head does a body." When Jesus took His

---

[24] There is an alternative view of the nature of Jesus' intercession offered by J. Oswald Sanders. I believe it is worth mentioning. Sanders writes, "His intercession is not vocal. It is not an audible saying of prayers. In his great annual act of intercession, Aaron uttered not one word... On the day of atonement it was the blood that spoke, not Aaron. It is the presence of our Intercessor, bearing in His body the evidence of His victory, that speaks for us." This is from his book, *Spiritual Maturity*, Moody Publishers, Chicago, Illinois, 1962, Page 110. Whatever Jesus' intercession entails, whether it involves spoken words or merely His Presence, we can be certain that it is sufficient.

rightful place beside the Father, He did not flop into a recliner to take a nap; He sits on a throne of authority, and He reigns as Lord of His Church.

Three examples of Jesus exercising His loving Lordship over the Church include the following:

❖ As Stephen, the first martyr of the Church, was being put to death, Jesus stood to honor and welcome him. As the angry mob began to attack him, Stephen, "being full of the Holy Spirit, gazed into heaven and saw the glory of God, and Jesus standing at the right hand of God, and said, 'Look! I see the heavens opened and the Son of Man standing at the right hand of God!'" (Acts 7:55–56).

❖ In Acts 9:1–5, Jesus made a special "recruiting trip" to call Saul of Tarsus unto Himself and to enlist him in Christian ministry.

❖ In the final book of the New Testament, Jesus reveals Himself as One who is walking in the midst of the churches, as One who is holding the messengers of the churches—the pastors—in His mighty right hand (Revelation 1:12–2:1).

4. Jesus Is Working Today as Our Healer.

Even a casual reading of the Gospels provides numerous examples of Jesus' works in healing. Since Jesus "is the same yesterday, today, and forever" (Hebrews 13:8), it should come as no surprise that Jesus still works today in the arena of healing.

❖ Mark made it very clear that Jesus did not discontinue His healing ministry after His ascension. Mark 16:20 says, "And the disciples went everywhere and preached, and the Lord worked through them, confirming what they said by many miraculous signs" (*NLT*).

❖ Peter said to the paralyzed man in Lydda, "Aeneas, Jesus the Christ heals you. Arise and make your bed" (Acts 9:34). Immediately the man was healed.

❖ James counseled believers, "Is anyone among you sick? Let him call for the elders of the church, and let them pray over him, anointing him with oil in the name of the Lord. And the prayer of faith will save the sick, and the Lord will raise him up" (James 5:14–15).

5. Jesus Is Working Today as the Sustainer and Perfecter.

In Hebrews 1:2–4, Jesus is referred to as the Son of God and the heir of all things. In addition to references to Jesus' past work (His role in creation and His role in redemption), we also read that Jesus is "upholding all things by the word of His power." *The Amplified Bible* says that Jesus is "upholding and maintaining and guiding and propelling the universe by His mighty word of power." This correlates to what Paul said of Jesus, that "He existed before anything else, and he holds all creation together" (Colossians 1:17, *NLT*).

Not only does Jesus have a present-day function of sustaining the universe, but He is also involved in perfecting us. Hebrews 12:2 tells us that we are to keep our eyes upon "Jesus, the author and finisher of our faith." Think about that. Jesus is not only the origin and source of our faith, but He is also the One who will perfect and bring to completion that which He started in our lives. The *New Living Translation* tells us that Jesus is "the champion who initiates and perfects our faith."

How Will Jesus Work in the Future?

Referring to the Messiah, Isaiah said, "Of the increase of His government and peace there will be no end" (Isaiah 9:7). I believe it is safe to say that the works of Christ are not only continuing today, but there are also vast future works yet to be seen. I can't begin to do justice to this wonderful thought—volumes have been written regarding eschatology (the doctrine of last things)—but be assured that Jesus has works yet to carry out, and they will be glorious. What will a few of these works look like?

❖ Jesus told His followers, "I go to prepare a place for you. And if I go and prepare a place for you, I will come again and receive you to Myself; that where I am, there you may be also" (John 14:2–3). We know that Jesus is preparing a place for us, and that He will come for us one day.

❖ Paul said that we are "looking for the blessed hope and glorious appearing of our great God and Savior Jesus Christ" (Titus 2:13). We know that Jesus will appear in the future.

❖ "For the Lord Himself will descend from heaven with a shout, with the voice of an archangel, and with the trumpet of God. And the dead in Christ will rise first. Then we who are alive and remain shall be caught up together with them in the clouds to meet the Lord in the air. And thus we shall always be with the Lord" (1 Thessalonians 4:16–17). We know that Jesus will oversee a great and glorious reunion.

❖ Paul said that Jesus will "transform our lowly body that it may be conformed to His glorious body, according to the working by which He is able even to subdue all things to Himself" (Philippians 3:21). *The Message* tells us that Jesus "will transform our earthy bodies into glorious bodies like his own. He'll make us beautiful and whole with the same powerful skill by which he is putting everything as it should be, under and around him." We know that Jesus will orchestrate a beautiful transformation—in us and in the earth.

❖ "For we must all appear and be revealed as we are before the judgment seat of Christ, so that each one may receive [his pay] according to what he has done in the body, whether good or evil [considering what his purpose and motive have been, and what he has achieved, been busy with, and given himself and his attention to accomplishing]" (2 Corinthians 5:10, *AMP*). We know that Jesus will one day conduct a great judgment.

❖ "The kingdoms of this world have become the kingdoms of our Lord and of His Christ, and He shall reign forever and ever!" (Revelation 11:15). We know that one of Jesus' future works is to reign forever!

When we consider all the works of Jesus—what He's done in the past, what He's doing in His present-day ministry, and what He is yet to do in the future—what does it mean to us? It means that each of us can say, "I trust and rest in the finished work that Christ accomplished for me. I yield to and cooperate with the ongoing work of Christ in me and through me. In addition, I dedicate myself to the unfinished task—the Great Commission—assigned to me by Christ, the Head of the Church. And finally, I anticipate the ultimate consummation of Christ's works in His eternal kingdom, when He will reign forever and ever."

Just like His Father, Jesus was and is a worker. This sets the stage for us to not only enjoy and benefit from all Their works, but to also begin to explore what Their working nature means in terms of who *we* were created to be and what *we* were created to do. As we come to know God more and more, we are drawn into His works, to be personally affected by them and to pattern our lives after His example.

Quotes Worth Remembering

"Sanctification is that inward spiritual work which the Lord Jesus Christ works in a man by the Holy Spirit when He calls him to be a true believer. He not only washes him from his sins in His own blood, but He also separates him from his natural love of sin and the world, puts a new principle in his heart and makes him practically godly in life."
—*J.C. Ryle*

"We believe that to Christ belongs creative power— that 'without Him was not anything made which was made.' We believe that from Him came all life at first. In Him life was as in its deep source. He is the fountain of life. We believe that as no being comes into existence without His creative power, so none continues to exist without His sustaining energy. We believe that the history of the world is but the history of His influence, and that the centre of the whole universe is the cross of Cavalry."
—*Alexander MacLaren*

"In His life Christ is an example, showing us how to live;
In His death He is a sacrifice, satisfying for our sins;
In His resurrection, a conqueror;
In His ascension, a king
In His intercession, a high priest."
—*Martin Luther*

Questions for Reflection and Discussion

1. Consider that the Messiah, the Savior of the world, engaged in common, everyday work. What does Jesus' profession as a carpenter say about Him and about work itself?

2. In this chapter, we read that works were not an option to Jesus, and that doing God's work brought Jesus great fulfillment. Why do you think Jesus had the kind of work ethic that He had, and how should Jesus' view of work affect and influence us?

3. Describe in your own words what it means when we refer to "the finished work of Christ." What is it that Jesus finished, and what does that aspect of His work mean to us today?

4. Review the five functions listed in the section "How Is Jesus Working Today?" Which of these roles and responsibilities that Jesus carries out has the most influence on your life? Which of these are you most mindful and aware of, and how do all of them impact your daily life?

5. How relevant are the future works of Christ to us today? How should what Jesus is going to do in the future affect how we see this world and the way we live in the present?

CHAPTER THREE

Why We Work:
Finding the Purpose

"Let every man abide in the calling wherein he is called and his work will
be as sacred as the work of the ministry. It is not what a man does that
determines whether his work is sacred or secular, it is why he does it."
—A.W. Tozer

I think the writers of the Westminster Shorter Catechism got it right when they stated, "Man's chief end is to glorify God, and to enjoy him forever."[25] But I can't help but think that working must fit somewhere into the equation. After all, having created man in His own image, God gives what could be described as the first "work assignment" in Genesis 1:28: "Be fruitful and multiply; fill the earth and subdue it; have dominion over the fish of the sea, over the birds of the air, and over every living thing that moves on the earth." Of this first assignment, M. D. Geldard offers the following explanation:

> Work—in the sense of taking charge of the environment, of maintaining, ordering, and organizing it—is thus fundamental to God's purposes for human life. Human work, as worship, is an

---

[25] *Westminster Shorter Catechism*, Westminster Assembly, 1647.

activity in which the divine image is set forth. Given the ancient Near Eastern context, rule (dominion) here is to be understood in terms of monarchy. Man is a king, set over nature by God. He is, therefore, the vice-regent, responsible to his Creator for how he uses and organizes the creation.[26]

Man had a purpose, something to apply himself to and accomplish, and this purpose is important.

Practically speaking, one of the first things God did when He placed man into the Garden was to give him an even more specific assignment—a job. In Genesis 2:15, we read that God "took the man and put him in the garden of Eden to tend and keep it." The word "tend" here literally means *to work*. It would seem that working is just one of the many ways that we were designed to fulfill God's plan for our lives, and by which we are to glorify Him on the earth.

Other translations render Adam's assignment as the following:

❖ "to cultivate it and guard it" (*GNB*)

❖ "to work it and keep it" (*ESV*)

❖ "to work it and take care of it" (*NIV*)

❖ "to farm the land and take care of it" (*GW*)

❖ "to work it and watch over it" (*HCSB*)

❖ "to care for it and to maintain it" (*NET*)

Consider these words: cultivate, guard, work, keep, take care of, farm, watch over, and maintain. Adam had a definitive job description, and everything he was assigned to do was based on God's instructions. In other words, his work was to be done as unto the Lord. *The Bible Knowledge*

---

[26] Harrison, R.K., Editor. *Encyclopedia of Biblical and Christian Ethics* (Nashville, Tennessee: Thomas Nelson Publishers, 1987), 443.

Commentary points out that God placed Adam in the garden, "to work it ('*ābad*, 'to serve') and to take care of it. Whatever work [Adam] did was therefore described as his service to God."[27]

As we learned in the first chapter, God evaluated all of His work in Genesis 1:31. His assessment? "God saw everything that He had made, and indeed it was very good." Since we have been created in the image and likeness of God (Genesis 1:26), it stands to reason that we are also called to do good works and to produce good things.

Some people have erroneously believed that man did not have to work until after the Fall, when sin came into the picture. But that's not true. Adam was given a job before the fall of man took place. Work, productivity, and purpose were part of God's plan for man from the very beginning. Sinclair B. Ferguson writes, "Twentieth-century man needs to be reminded at times that work is not the result of the Fall. Man was made to work, because the God who made him was a 'working God.' Man was made to be creative, with his mind and his hands. Work is part of the dignity of his existence."[28] Larry Peabody further explains the notion of work this way:

> Work is not a punishment for man's wrongdoing. It originated as a continuation, an extension of God's activity. God's works are so many and so varied no man can number them. God, the Worker, created in His image man, the worker. This makes working a privilege, an honor. In working, we are doing what our heavenly Father has done since the beginning.[29]

---

[27] Ross, Allen P. "Genesis", *The Bible Knowledge Commentary: An Exposition of the Scriptures*, ed. J. F. Walvoord and R. B. Zuck (Wheaton, IL: Victor Books, 1985). Genesis 2:15–17.

[28] Ferguson, Sinclair B. *A Heart for God*, (Edinburgh, Scotland: Banner of Truth, 1987).

[29] Peabody, Larry. *Serving Christ in the Workplace: Secular Work is Full-time Service* (Fort Washington, PA: CLC Publications, 2004.) Used by permission of CLC Publications. May not be further reproduced. All rights reserved.

It's true that work became more complicated and more frustrating after the fall (Genesis 3:17–19), but it wasn't a by-product of sin.

Adam and Eve's children worked as well; "Abel was a herdsman and Cain a farmer" (Genesis 4:2, *MSG*). Abel must have seen a connection between his work and worship, because in Genesis 4:4 we read, "Abel also brought of the firstborn of his flock and of their fat. And the Lord respected Abel and his offering." In Hebrews 11:4, we read that Abel's offering, which he brought in faith, was "a more excellent" sacrifice than Cain's. Is there a lesson here for us? Are we to see our entire lives, including the works of our hands, as an offering unto God? Are we called to present to God by faith all that we are, all that we have, and all that we do as expressions of worship? This understanding could revolutionize the way believers see their work. Instead of seeing work as drudgery, we can see all that we do—all of the work of our hands and our minds—as worship unto the Lord.

God's People Were Designed to Be Workers

It is helpful for us to have an accurate understanding of exactly what work is, and it is imperative that we allow the Word and wisdom of God to form the basis of our perception. It is going to be hard to have a godly understanding of why we work if our very definition of work is one that is corrupted by cynicism and negativity.

Instead, we need to see work as a way to reflect the dignity and virtue inherent in God's purpose for our lives. William J. Bennett, former Secretary of Education under President Reagan, writes, "Work is applied effort; it is whatever we put ourselves into, whatever we expend our energy on for the sake of accomplishing or achieving something. Work in this fundamental sense is not what we do *for* a living but what we do *with* our living."[30] Adding a spiritual component, the English Evangelical leader, John Stott defines work as "the expenditure of energy (manual or mental or both) in the service of others, which brings fulfillment to the worker, benefit to the community, and glory to God."[31] And what are some of the end results of our work? In *Your Work Matters to God*, the following purposes are identified:

1. Through work we serve people.

2. Through work we meet our own needs.

3. Through work we meet our family's needs.

4. Through work we earn money to give to others.

5. Through work we love others.[32]

How do *you* see work? Do you see it as a burden or a blessing? Do you approach work with grumbling or with thanksgiving? D. Elton Trueblood writes, "Wherever the gospel has been truly influential the concept of the dignity of work has emerged. The change from the conception of work as a curse to work as partnership with God owes more than we ordinarily realize to the witness of Christ."[33] If we have a good understanding of what work really is—and what God designed it to be—we will have a much better chance of having the right attitude toward what we do.

Whether the job is what people would call "secular work" (nurses, construction workers, bankers, and so forth) or "religious work" (pastors, evangelists, missionaries, and so forth), God's people were designed to be productive and diligent workers. One of the challenges Christians have

---

[30] Bennett, William J. *The Book of Virtues* (New York, New York: Simon & Schuster, 1993), 347.
[31] Stott, John. *Issues Facing Christians Today* (Grand Rapids, Michigan: Zondervan, 2006), 225.
[32] Taken from *Your Work Matters to God* by Doug Sherman and William Hendricks. Copyright © 1987 by NavPress. Used by permission of Tyndale House Publishers, Inc. All rights reserved.
[33] Henry, Carl F.H. editor. *Baker's Dictionary of Christian Ethics* (Grand Rapids, Michigan: Baker Book House, 1973), 714.

when it comes to work is the mindset that secular work is somehow inferior to and less important than religious work. However, many forms of work—not just what people consider spiritual or ministerial work—are positively represented in Scripture.

Even though the Bible presents many spiritual truths, it also deals extensively with the day-to-day, practical responsibilities of life. Joel L. Meredith points out that Scripture identifies 198 different vocations, including barbers, cooks, fishermen, merchants, miners, physicians, scientists, and tax collectors.[34] Authors Trull and Carter expound on the divine calling present in secular vocations in the following text:

> Before the Reformation it was generally believed that the only people who received a divine calling were those chosen by God to enter the spiritually superior monastic way. This calling (*vocatio*) was reserved for religious professionals alone. Martin Luther and John Calvin challenged this tradition, basing their argument on the biblical teaching of calling prominent in the Pauline epistles (Romans 12:6-8; 1 Corinthians 7:20-24; 12:28; Ephesians 4:11). Both Reformers asserted that every worthwhile form of work was a divine calling. The farmer, the merchant, and the cobbler, not just the priest, had a call from God to serve the world in their work."[35]

We would do well to recognize God's presence and power available to equip us for our work, regardless of the type of job we have. His ultimate purpose for our life remains the same, and we can be a witness for Him in our profession even if our career is outside our church. Martin Luther explains this truth in clear terms:

---

[34] Meredith, Joel L. *Meredith's Complete Book of Bible Lists* (Minneapolis: Bethany House Publishers, 2009.

[35] Trull, Joe E. and Carter, James E. *Ministerial Ethics* (Grand Rapids, Michigan: Baker Academic, a division of Baker Publishing Group, 2004.

The idea that the service to God should have only to do with a church altar, singing, reading, sacrifice, and the like is without doubt but the worst trick of the devil. How could the devil have led us more effectively astray than by the narrow conception that service to God takes place only in a church and by the works done therein. . . . The whole world could abound with the services to the Lord . . . not only in churches but also in the home, kitchen, workshop, field.

As our nation was forming, influence from Luther's Protestant Reformation affected the way people viewed their work. Historical research shows the important influence of the Puritan, or Protestant, work ethic: "The belief that (1) man is called to work, (2) all work has a sense of nobility, and (3) a Christian serves God best by working diligently and faithfully in his calling. Although the Puritan work ethic was later secularized (removed from its religious roots), it became an important part of the American character and laid the groundwork for a prosperous economy."[36] This idea of being called, of finding a sense of nobility in one's work, and the connection between work ethic and service to God isn't something that we should relegate to the Puritans. This concept is firmly grounded in Scripture and still applies to us today.

While we understand that there are inherent differences in the type of work people do, all work that is moral, ethical, and helpful to others can be done for the glory of God. Furthermore, the work can be done without any demoralizing thought that one's work is somehow less significant because it has been labeled as secular. I agree with A.W. Tozer, who believed that sanctified Christians living sanctified lives will, in a sense, then sanctify their work:

[36] Grussendorf, Kurt A., Michael R. Lowman and Brian S. Ashbaugh. *America: Land I Love, Second Edition* (Pensacola, Florida: A Beka Book, 2006), 36.

Let us think of a Christian believer in whose life the twin wonders of repentance and the new birth have been wrought. He is now living according to the will of God as he understands it from the written Word. Of such a one it may be said that every act of his life is or can be as truly sacred as prayer or baptism or the Lord's Supper. To say this is not to bring all acts down to one dead level; it is rather to lift every act up into a living kingdom and turn the whole of life into a sacrament.

It is important that we identify and recognize the intrinsic value of work, even though the actual work itself might not be deemed spiritual in nature. Just as God worked to provide spiritual blessings through Jesus, He also labored to provide natural blessings such as oxygen and sunlight through Creation. We, too, can perform spiritual or natural work with significance. When people labor honorably, they provide necessary goods and important services for others.

❖ The work of farmers provides food for people.

❖ Mechanics keep people's cars running.

❖ Doctors help keep people healthy.

❖ Teachers help educate society.

❖ Custodians and housekeepers keep businesses clean.

❖ Servers in restaurants deliver meals to people.

❖ Plumbers and electricians keep our homes supplied with water and power.

❖ Civil authorities keep order in society. As a matter of fact, Romans 13:4 says, "The authorities are God's servants, sent for your good" (*NLT*).

❖ Factory workers produce various kinds of products for consumers.

❖ Truck drivers deliver needed goods to people.

All of these and many other types of work provide for the common good. Clearly, the "natural" abilities necessary for these functions to be carried out are an expression of God's wise plan for our needs to be met. When people in these various vocations do work that benefits us, we can be grateful to them *and* grateful to God. Also, when we utilize *our* gifts in serving others, we can see ourselves using our God-given abilities to serve humanity. You don't have to feel like a second-class citizen in God's family if your gifting and functioning is in one of these (or many other) practical areas.

It is unfortunate that some people still seem to think that only preachers engage in ultimately worthwhile activities. This is simply not the case. First, preachers are not the only ones who deal with spiritual and eternal matters. Anyone can minister at their job, showing God's love by example, praying with and for coworkers, being kind to a colleague, or telling others about Christ. Second, while God cares about and has made provision for meeting our spiritual needs, He also cares about and provides to meet our natural needs. If every person on earth was a preacher, how would we eat? No farmers, no merchants, no chefs? The world of preachers would starve!

Many of the people we consider to be great heroes of faith were not preachers per se. Though they may at times have shared a message or written something highly significant, in their everyday lives they were busy doing what people would call secular work.

Abraham was an influential tribal leader, powerful herdsman, and trader. Genesis 13:2 says, "Abram was very rich, loaded with cattle and silver and gold" (*MSG*). While we don't know Abraham's exact net worth, we know that when his nephew Lot was taken captive, he "armed his three hundred and eighteen trained servants who were born in his own house, and went in pursuit" (Genesis 14:14). If that many servants were trained in arms and capable of going to war, it is reasonable to assume that Abraham probably had more than one thousand servants overall. How many people do you know who have one thousand employees? Later, we read that Abraham's servant said of him, "The LORD has blessed my master greatly, and he has become great; and He has given him flocks and herds, silver and gold, male and female servants, and camels and donkeys" (Genesis 24:35). Though Abraham's enterprise was nomadic in nature, he would still have been considered a CEO by today's standards.

In Exodus 18:20, God told Moses (who had been a shepherd for forty years), "And you shall teach them the statutes and the laws, and show them the way in which they must walk and the work they must do." Notice that Moses was to teach and to show the people "the work they must do." There was value in the work God's people did in Exodus, and there is value in the work that God's people do today.

Joseph was another well-known non-preacher. His résumé includes such titles as household slave, prisoner, prison manager, and government official. God directed Joseph and gave him wisdom to function wisely in every role. Joseph's faithfulness led to his ultimate promotion to governor of Egypt, second in command beneath Pharaoh. From that governmental position, Joseph not only served the nation of Egypt, but he was also instrumental in ensuring Israel's survival through severe famine.

When we first meet Daniel, he is a student, but we eventually see him as a high-ranking government official—a statesman and administrator— in the Babylonian and Persian empires. Though Daniel was a prophet, he also diligently discharged his political and managerial responsibilities. In

Daniel 2:48, we read that "the king promoted Daniel and gave him many great gifts; and he made him ruler over the whole province of Babylon, and chief administrator over all the wise men of Babylon."

Nehemiah's secular work was also very significant in preparing him for and launching him into the assignment God had for him. Nehemiah served the Persian king Artaxerxes as his cupbearer. One commentary says of this, "This officer, in the ancient Oriental courts, was always a person of rank and importance; and, from the confidential nature of his duties and his frequent access to the royal presence, he possessed great influence."[37] This influence and the skills Nehemiah learned from his time serving the king helped prepare him to lead Israel when God called.

God gave Nehemiah the monumental task of rebuilding the destroyed walls of Jerusalem after the Babylonian captivity. Wisely, Nehemiah organized and delegated the responsibilities among the people. Even Israel's enemies were surprised how quickly the wall was rebuilt. Nehemiah 4:6 reveals the secret of their effectiveness, saying, "So we built the wall, and the entire wall was joined together up to half its height, *for the people had a mind to work*" (emphasis mine).

Good things happen when people work, especially when they work in unison and with a godly purpose. While our focus in this book is largely upon the efforts of the individual, let's remember the phenomenal results that occur when there is *team*work taking place. In addition to being great workers, it's also important that we become great team members.

It is interesting to note, though, that not everyone in Jerusalem applied himself and carried his weight. Nehemiah 3:5 says, "Next to them the Tekoites made repairs; but their nobles did not put their shoulders to the work of their Lord." The fact that this verse specifies that the non-workers

---

[37] Jamieson, Robert, A. R. Fausset and David Brown. *Commentary Critical and Explanatory on the Whole Bible* (Oak Harbor, WA: Logos Research Systems, Inc., 1997).

were nobles indicates to me that perhaps they felt they were too good to work, or that physical labor was beneath their station. The *English Standard Version* translates this verse, "Their nobles would not stoop to serve their Lord." Whatever the reason, their refusal to work and their lack of contribution was noted by many.

As for Jerusalem after the captivity, the rebuilding of the walls was not the first time the people had been rallied to work. Earlier, the prophet Haggai had spoken to the people about the need to rebuild the temple. He said, "'Be strong, all you people of the land,' says the LORD, 'and work; for I am with you,' says the LORD of hosts" (Haggai 2:4). Note that in this case, God's presence did not preclude the need to work, but was actually the basis for working.

Many people we read about in the New Testament had everyday jobs as well:

❖ In addition to being a doctor, Luke "the beloved physician" was the author of the Gospel bearing his name and the Book of Acts, and he was also a very faithful friend and traveling companion of the Apostle Paul (Colossians 4:14). One commentary suggests renderings such as, "Luke who is our dear doctor," or "Luke, our doctor, who is dear to us," or "Luke, who is so much appreciated by us."[38] When you consider all of the beatings, imprisonments, shipwrecks, and so forth that Paul experienced, it is likely that Luke utilized some of his medical skills to care for Paul after these traumatic events. If such care in fact took place, this could account for Paul's expression of endearment and appreciation.

---

[38] Bratcher, Robert G. and Eugene Albert Nida. *A Handbook on Paul's Letters to the Colossians and to Philemon.* UBS Handbook Series (New York: United Bible Societies, 1993).

❖ Lydia, Paul's first convert in Europe and the host to Paul's team, was described as a "merchant of expensive purple cloth" (Acts 16:14–15, *NLT*). By all indications, Lydia was a well-to-do businesswoman and after her conversion, she hosted Paul and his apostolic team during their stay in Philippi.

❖ One of Paul's friends and associates, Erastus, also served as the city treasurer of Corinth (Acts 19:22; Romans 16:23; 2 Timothy 4:20). Based on archaeological evidence, F.F. Bruce suggests, "Erastus perhaps made good as city treasurer; we find him later occupying a higher position in the civic administration—the position of adeile (curator of public works)."[39]

To assign various forms of work the value and dignity they deserve, it is important to realize that God not only has eternal and heavenly plans for His people, but He also has temporal and earthly plans. God wisely gave people a variety of wisdom and aptitudes so that a wide range of needs can be met. This is why many activities that are often labeled as "secular" can be vital and honorable expressions of God's care for those He created and loves. The biblical examples who worked according to their giftings and assignments participated in God's plans being furthered, and humanity was served through their work upon this earth.

While some individuals may have continued their everyday work throughout their lives, others discontinued their regular work when God gave them another task. For example, most people know that four of the disciples Jesus recruited (Peter, Andrew, James, and John) had been fishermen, and Matthew had been a tax collector. They left their work to be disciples. We don't know how long he continued the non-ministry aspects of his work, but the Old Testament prophet Amos said, "I'm not a

---

[39] Bruce, F.F. *The Pauline Circle* (Eugene, Oregon: Wipf & Stock Publishers, 1985), 88.

professional prophet, and I was never trained to be one. I'm just a shepherd, and I take care of sycamore-fig trees" (Amos 7:14, *NLT*).

Paul's Example

In chapter two, we discussed the fact that before he entered ministry, Jesus worked as a carpenter. It would be good to also address the secular vocation of another great spiritual leader—the Apostle Paul. Paul is known for his tireless labor of traveling, starting churches, and writing divinely inspired epistles. But less well known is the fact that Paul often and frequently engaged in secular work in conjunction with his travels and ministry.

The first indication of Paul's vocational background occurs in Corinth after Paul meets Priscilla and Aquila. We read that "Paul lived and worked with them, for they were tentmakers just as he was" (Acts 18:3, *NLT*). One commentary says, "A number of the early church fathers rendered the term used here by a more general word, 'leather worker.' This is quite plausible. Tents were often made of leather, and tentmakers probably used their skills on other types of leather products as well."[40] Today, people would say that Paul was bi-vocational because he both preached and did secular work. He alluded to his secular work in various instances:

- ❖ "These hands of mine have worked to supply my own needs and even the needs of those who were with me. And I have been a constant example of how you can help those in need by working hard" (Acts 20:34–35, *NLT*).

- ❖ "And we labor, working with our own hands" (1 Corinthians 4:12).

---

[40] Polhill, John B. "Acts." *The New American Commentary* (Nashville: Broadman & Holman Publishers, 1992).

❖ "Don't you remember, dear brothers and sisters, how hard we worked among you? Night and day we toiled to earn a living so that we would not be a burden to any of you as we preached God's Good News to you" (1 Thessalonians 2:9, *NLT*).

❖ "We never accepted food from anyone without paying for it. We worked hard day and night so we would not be a burden to any of you" (2 Thessalonians 3:8, *NLT*).

Why did Paul work? Because he felt it was his responsibility to set a great example by supplying his own needs so that he would not be a burden to others. I believe that whether Paul was preaching or making tents, he did it all for the glory of God and the benefit of others. S.J. Mikolaski explains this concept in detail:

Three important principles follow from biblical teaching. First, as much as lies within their power, each Christian and Christian family should strive to be self-reliant. This is not merely to avoid becoming a drain on others, but to produce more than their own needs so that others can share in the abundance. Second, Christians should strive for excellence. When men and women do good work and produce dependable products, they bless and enrich the lives of others. Third, Christians ought to strive to improve the world, making it a better place than it was when they came into it.[41]

Mikolaski concludes his thoughts saying, "As a general rule, therefore, the Christian ought to work hard in a useful vocation, striving to contribute to the good of humanity."[42] Paul's motivation should be our motivation.

Why do we work? We bear the image of God in the earth. We are to embody His creative, productive, life-giving nature to those around us.

---

[41] Harrison, R.K. editor. *Encyclopedia of Biblical and Christian Ethics* (Nashville, Tennessee: Thomas Nelson Publishers, 1987), 432–433.
[42] ibid, 433.

Work, properly seen, is a gift from God, an avenue through which needs can be met and from which generosity can flow. Above all, work is just one of the many ways in which we are to glorify God.

Quotes Worth Remembering

*"We meet God the Creator as a worker in Genesis 1:1–2:2. God being a worker
endows all legitimate work with an intrinsic dignity. The way we work will
reveal how much we have allowed the image of God to develop in us.
There is immense dignity in work and in being workers."*
—R. Kent Hughes

*"All labor that uplifts humanity has dignity and importance
and should be undertaken with excellence."*
—Martin Luther King Jr.

"Oh, give us the man who sings at his work."
—Thomas Carlyle

"We work to become, not to acquire."
—Elbert Hubbard

*"No man needs sympathy because he has to work. . . .
Far and away the best prize that life offers is the chance
to work hard at work worth doing."*
—Theodore Roosevelt

Questions for Reflection and Discussion

1. How have you viewed work over the years? What has your attitude toward work been? Has it been better at certain times than at other times? What caused the difference in perspectives?

2. How clear is your sense of purpose in life? Do you believe that you are glorifying God and serving others through the way you work—on the job and otherwise?

3. Review the definitions of work by William Bennett and John Stott. Which parts of these definitions speak the most to you? If you were to write your own definition of work, what would it be?

4. In this chapter, I cited Luther and Calvin, who "asserted that every worthwhile form of work was a divine calling." Do you agree or disagree with this assertion? What is the basis for your perspective? How does this apply to you and your life?

5. Make a mental list of the people whose work enhances and enriches your life. If you are in a group, share this list with your group. How does their work make your life better? Are you actively thankful for these people and what they do, or do you tend to take their work for granted?

REFLECTIONS FROM READERS

Jennifer from Minnesota writes:

My work ethic was instilled in me by my parents, who got it from theirs and so on. My parents always endeavored to serve well no matter whether it was at work, church, volunteering, or with their family. They met their obligations. They put God first in it all, and that is what I try to do as well.

I have a benefactor personality that loves to help, which is evident by the various occupations I've had, from a lobbyist working to improve communities around our state to a realtor helping people find the home perfect for their family. I also have a strong desire to see my family live very comfortably and to be able to give to others, my church, and my community. That drives me to work hard to earn money. God has blessed me with the skills to help others and an opportunity to make money doing so, and I have an obligation to use those skills and abilities.

My time is limited, but I find that when I put God first and take time to spend with Him, other things seem to go much more smoothly, increasing my productivity. Proverbs is filled with verses that motivate me—verses about working hard, working wisely, and living a balanced life. I get energy from being productive and prioritizing. And I like closure and completion! I gain fulfillment from the happiness that I see on clients' faces at closing and from hearing the way they talk about me to others. I have learned that when I focus on what

REFLECTIONS FROM READERS

I can give, there is so much that I receive—both naturally and spiritually.

Mark from Alabama writes:

The reason I work hard and do so effectively is because I have never known any other way to work. I was brought up by two hardworking parents who managed to raise four children while working full-time jobs and keeping a small farm. I grew up in a household where hard work was the norm, and since I was the oldest son, I spent most of my time working alongside my father.

My father instilled four things within me, and these four principles enable me to work efficiently and effectively.

The first principle my father instilled in me is that a man's work is a reflection of that man; therefore, it is important to do your best at all times no matter the task. It did not matter if my father was mending a fence or machining a part for the space shuttle; he was going to do his best.

The second thing instilled in me by my father is the importance of taking care of all that the Lord has given. I have not only witnessed my father giving his family the best of care, but I have also witnessed him doing the same for his animals, cars, tools, etc. If he was in the middle of working on an outdoor project and it became too dark for him to finish, he never left any of his tools or equipment outdoors. He always picked everything up and put them away until the next day.

REFLECTIONS FROM READERS

The third principle I learned from my father is the importance of being organized. I never saw my father waste time looking for any of his tools. Every item in his shop had a place. He always put things back where he found them, and he expected his children to follow suit.

The fourth thing instilled in me by my father is the importance of being on time. He never liked to waste his own time, so he did not think it was right to waste someone else's time.

Amanda from Missouri writes:

First, I have to give credit to my parents (probably a lot more credit than I know). They are both very diligent, faithful people who have been very steady in their secular jobs and service to the Lord. From a young age, they instilled in us a healthy respect for work and the importance of a job well done. We were brought up to believe that work is a normal, everyday part of life.

So why work so hard and effectively? This is the part that has evolved through the years. At first, it was a kind of inward drive to be the best student, the best athlete, the best employee, etc. I wanted to be "at the top," so I would study hard, practice hard, and so forth to try to obtain that high place (really, this was just a form of pride). The affirmation of those in authority reassured me and played a part in my continual focus on excellence and wanting to "keep up the good work." I guess you could say that I started out internally motivated by external factors and conditions. But that has changed now.

I don't mean to over-spiritualize anything, but I have come to a place where the reason that I do what I do is simply because I believe that my work is my assignment from the Lord. *He* values the place and position that He gave me—in my job and in my service at church—therefore, *I* value it. It has Kingdom significance, which is a greater value than I could attach to it on my own. As much as I desire to be pleasing to those in authority over me, I desire it all the more with the Lord.

If my heart is fixed on the Lord, then it won't matter so much what those around me do or don't do. I can stay the course, be steady, and continue to work hard knowing that what I am doing has value, no matter how insignificant it might seem. Why do I find my work so fulfilling? Because I believe in my heart that the Lord gave it to me. It's a gift. It's no longer about me and what I can accomplish or about my striving to get to the top (wherever that is); it's about finding my place, staying in my lane, and finishing what the Lord has given me to do at my job, at home, and at church. I think a lot more now about "the whole," or what we are accomplishing together. Who are we affecting? Who are we helping? This motivates me to be as diligent, resourceful, efficient, and effective as I can be. There is a job to get done. There is work to do. But it isn't a competition, and it isn't mine alone.

Cindy from Oklahoma writes:

I know how and am willing to put my shoulder to the task in any situation where the Lord requires my effort and my skills. But I've found that what sustains and strengthens me to go the extra mile again and again is the knowledge that I'm working for a God-ordained purpose that ignites a fire in my heart. The clock loses significance in the light of that inner fire! It fuels me when I know God has positioned me to help fulfill a task or assignment, and His desires for that assignment have become mine as well.

I draw on God's grace and strength to do what is necessary to fulfill my part so I can stay aligned to the path He has ordained for me. Something my pastor once said along this line struck a chord in me because I so identified with it: "When you have a cause, you don't need excuses. You just fire it up and burn it on. You just keep going, keep going, keep going—everything you do just flows out of you!" So my work ethic flows from my cause, which is to do what God has ordained for me to do to further His purposes to the glory of Jesus.

CHAPTER FOUR

How We Work: Rolling Up Our Sleeves and Getting the Job Done

We pray that you'll live well for the Master, making him proud of you as you
work hard in his orchard. As you learn more and more how God works,
you will learn how to do your work.
—Colossians 1:10 (MSG)

Grit. It's a word we don't hear very much these days. A dictionary defines "grit" as *firmness of mind or spirit: unyielding courage in the face of hardship or danger.*[43] One dictionary illustrated the toughness and tenacity this word conveys in the following example phrase: "Through resourcefulness and grit, the pioneers survived the winter."[44] In other words, grit is necessary to making it through tough times and getting things done.

When I think of grit, I think about the Old Testament story of Eleazar, one of David's warriors. Second Samuel 23:10 says, "He killed Philistines until his hand was too tired to lift his sword, and the LORD gave him a great victory that day. The rest of the army did not return until it was time

---

[43] Merriam-webster online, s.v. "grit," http://www.merriam-webster.com/dictionary/grit.
[44] ibid

to collect the plunder!" (*NLT*). Eleazar fought until he could fight no more. And where were his brothers-in-arms? They didn't show up until the battle was over!

Eleazar's experience reminds me of the story many of us read as a child called *The Little Red Hen*. The little red hen lived with a duck, a pig, and a cat. The hen found a grain of corn, planted it, harvested it, took the kernels to be turned into flour, and made the flour into bread. At every step, she asked the others if they would help her, and she always received a negative response. However, when she sat down to eat the bread, everyone else wanted to partake. The story perfectly illustrates how people love the event (the finished product), but don't necessarily want to contribute during the process.

Tenacity and perseverance are important qualities. If we don't quit, we will go far in life. One of the stories Rev. Kenneth E. Hagin shared with us as young Bible school students illustrates the need to trust God to give us strength to complete difficult tasks. Having been healed after being bedfast for more than a year, Hagin had only been up and around for a couple of months. Those were Depression days, and work was hard to find. However, he got a job at a local nursery, pulling up two-year-old peach trees to fill purchase orders.

In his book *Exceedingly Growing Faith*, Hagin writes, "Each morning before sunup we would meet, and every day some of the boys would say, 'Well, I didn't think you'd make it today. You know, two or three quit yesterday.'

"'If it weren't for the Lord I wouldn't be here,' I would answer, for you see, His strength is my strength. The Bible says, 'The Lord is the strength of my life.'"

Hagin further explains, "Now, if I had gone by my feelings I would never have gotten out of bed! I was never so weak in my life. I felt as if I couldn't do it. But I stayed with it. I acted upon the Word because I knew what faith was."

Brother Hagin ends his testimony about his early work experience by saying, "When we began to work each morning I wouldn't have any strength, but when we started on the first tree (or sometimes the second) I would feel something hit me in the top of my head. It would go through my body, out the ends of my fingers, and out the ends of my toes. Then I would work all day long like a Trojan.... In the natural I was the weakest and the skinniest, but I was the only man left of the original crew. I had proved God's Word."[45]

You may read that testimony and have no interest in grueling, backbreaking, manual labor, but *whatever* we do—whether it is manual or intellectual labor, whether it is considered blue collar, white collar, or whatever collar—we should be diligent in our work and trust God to give us the strength and the wisdom to do what we need to do.

Proverbs Commends Diligence and Condemns Laziness

Ecclesiastes 9:10 admonishes, "Whatever your hand finds to do, do it with your might."

Tenacity, perseverance, diligence—these are not traits of the lazy. These are characteristics of the wise worker, the one who finds success. The Book of Proverbs deals extensively with wisdom, integrity, and moral uprightness. It contains very practical instruction, and work-related issues

---

[45] Hagin, Kenneth E. *Exceedingly Growing Faith* (Tulsa, Oklahoma: Faith Library Publications, 1983), 13-15.

permeate the book. We're told that the book was written "to give prudence to the simple, to the young man knowledge and discretion" (Proverbs 1:4).

Here are a few examples from Proverbs where the virtues of hard work are extolled, and the desolation resulting from laziness is exposed.

PROVERBS 6:6-11

6 Go to the ant, you sluggard! Consider her ways and be wise,

7 Which, having no captain, overseer or ruler,

8 Provides her supplies in the summer, and gathers her food in the harvest.

9 How long will you slumber, O sluggard? When will you rise from your sleep?

10 A little sleep, a little slumber, a little folding of the hands to sleep—

11 So shall your poverty come on you like a prowler, and your need like an armed man.

PROVERBS 10:4-5

4 He who has a slack hand becomes poor, but the hand of the diligent makes rich.

5 He who gathers in summer is a wise son; He who sleeps in harvest is a son who causes shame.

PROVERBS 10:16

The labor of the righteous leads to life, the wages of the wicked to sin.

PROVERBS 12:11 (*NLT*)

A hard worker has plenty of food, but a person who chases fantasies has no sense.

PROVERBS 12:24 (*NLT*)

Work hard and become a leader; be lazy and become a slave.

PROVERBS 12:27 (*MSG*)

A lazy life is an empty life, but "early to rise" gets the job done.

PROVERBS 13:4

The soul of a lazy man desires, and has nothing; but the soul of the diligent shall be made rich.

PROVERBS 13:11

Wealth gained by dishonesty will be diminished, but he who gathers by labor will increase.

PROVERBS 14:23

In all labor there is profit, but idle chatter leads only to poverty.

PROVERBS 20:24 (*NLT*)

Those too lazy to plow in the right season will have no food at the harvest.

PROVERBS 21:25

The desire of the lazy man kills him, for his hands refuse to labor.

PROVERBS 22:29

Do you see a man who excels in his work? He will stand before kings; He will not stand before unknown men.

PROVERBS 24:30-34

30 I went by the field of the lazy man, and by the vineyard of the man devoid of understanding;

31 And there it was, all overgrown with thorns; its surface was covered with nettles; its stone wall was broken down.

32 When I saw it, I considered it well; I looked on it and received instruction:

33 A little sleep, a little slumber, a little folding of the hands to rest;

34 So shall your poverty come like a prowler, and your need like an armed man.

PROVERBS 28:19 (*NLT*)
A hard worker has plenty of food, but a person who chases fantasies ends up in poverty.

PROVERBS 31:13, 27, 31
13 She seeks wool and flax, and willingly works with her hands.
27 She watches over the ways of her household, and does not eat the bread of idleness.
31 Give her of the fruit of her hands, and let her own works praise her in the gates.

Are these instructions realistic? Do people really work this hard? Obviously, some don't. But the Bible makes it clear that if we want to be wise and if we want to be successful in life, we will follow these instructions.

Translating These Admonitions into Practice

How do these instructions manifest in everyday life? What kinds of traits would a modern worker have if he or she were translating these admonitions from Proverbs into practice on the job? First let's look at the antithesis of a "Proverbs employee."

Many employers have observed a declining work ethic among employees, and others have seen a rise in a sense of entitlement among people in general. Some have told me that they are surprised at the questions they receive from potential employees. They reveal that candidates' questions during the job interview make it abundantly clear that the candidates want *a job*, so to speak, but they don't actually want *to work*—or at least not very hard. Apart from pay rate and the money to be made, primary interests of potential employees seem to focus on the following topics:

❖ How late can I come in?

❖ How early can I leave?

❖ How long can I take for lunch?

❖ How much time-off can I take?

❖ How much vacation time do I get?

Needless to say, these candidates often have to keep looking (and looking) for a job because they aren't the type of worker that employers want to hire.

One of the most important things a young person can acquire is a strong work ethic. My friend Pastor Gerald Brooks once told me, "For years, I have told young people entering the work force that if they will do these five things, they will be in the top 10% of workers in America:

❖ Show up.

❖ Show up on time.

❖ Show up prepared.

❖ Show up to do your best.

❖ Show up, and do the job for Jesus."

These principles, along with those in Proverbs, will equip you to be the kind of employee that companies and organizations will be scrambling to hire.

What Paul Taught About Work

Good advice on the subject of work isn't limited to the Old Testament. The Apostle Paul had many exemplary things to say about work.

One of the churches Paul started was located in Thessalonica, in northern Greece. Some of the believers there had the idea that Jesus was coming back so imminently that they quit their jobs and began mooching off of others. Paul admonished them, "Make it your goal to live a quiet life, minding your own business and working with your hands, just as we instructed you before. Then people who are not Christians will respect the way you live, and you will not need to depend on others" (1 Thessalonians 4:11-12, *NLT*). Shortly after this, he said, "We urge you to warn those who are lazy" (1 Thessalonians 5:14, *NLT*).

When Paul wrote his second epistle to this church, there were problems with people who lacked a good work ethic. Perhaps they thought the Lord was coming back so quickly that it was not important to work, or perhaps they just liked living off of the generosity of others. Paul had stern words for able-bodied individuals who were unwilling to work:

> Even while we were with you, we gave you this command: 'Those unwilling to work will not get to eat.' Yet we hear that some of you are living idle lives, refusing to work and meddling in other people's business. We command such people and urge them in the name of the Lord Jesus Christ to settle down and work to earn their own living (2 Thessalonians 3:10-12, *NLT*).

The Message version gives a very colorful rendering of this section of Scripture:

> And now we're getting reports that a bunch of lazy good-for-nothings are taking advantage of you. This must not be tolerated.

We command them to get to work immediately—no excuses, no arguments—and earn their own keep. Friends, don't slack off in doing your duty. If anyone refuses to obey our clear command written in this letter, don't let him get by with it. Point out such a person and refuse to subsidize his freeloading. Maybe then he'll think twice. But don't treat him as an enemy. Sit him down and talk about the problem as someone who cares (2 Thessalonians 3:11-15).

Paul was not talking about people who were disabled or who had not been able to work because of factors beyond their control; rather, he was addressing people who were unwilling to do what they could to help themselves. In Ephesians 4:28, he said, "Let him who stole steal no longer, but rather let him labor, working with his hands what is good, that he may have something to give him who has need." This idea of the less fortunate benefitting from our work existed long before the New Testament. Leviticus 23:22 says, "When you harvest the crops of your land, do not harvest the grain along the edges of your fields, and do not pick up what the harvesters drop. Leave it for the poor and the foreigners living among you. I am the LORD your God" (*NLT*).[46] When we've been blessed with a healthy body and a sound mind, we should work hard to provide for ourselves and also be happy to share our resources with those who are less fortunate and not able to take care of themselves.

When Paul addressed the church in Colosse, he encouraged servants to exhibit a good work ethic: "Servants, do what you're told by your earthly masters. And don't just do the minimum that will get you by. Do your best. Work from the heart for your real Master, for God, confident that you'll get paid in full when you come into your inheritance. Keep in mind always that the ultimate Master you're serving is Christ" (Colossians 3:22–24,

---

[46] See also Deuteronomy 24:19-22.

MSG). People who are diligently and faithfully serving God will make it a priority to have great attitudes on the job and will display an excellent work ethic. Even though they may have earthly supervisors and managers, these people realize that they are ultimately working for the glory and honor of God. This realization will cause them to give their best.

Displaying God's Purpose in Our Work

Not only does our work serve and help others, but *the way* we work—the attitude, integrity, and character we demonstrate—also offers a positive Christian witness. Pastor Jim Cobrae explains how our work displays God's purpose:

> Over the years, I have taught people that they are full-time ministers of Jesus Christ. God has called every person who is born of the Spirit of God to be a full-time minister. God just dresses these people up every week and sends them into the work place. Some of them put on their painters' outfits and become house painters. Another one may be a nurse and wears scrubs. Another guy works for the fire department, and God dresses him up.

> At the end of the week, they get a paycheck. But during that week, that's their ministry. And during that week they are to act out the Word; they are to be encouraging to people around them. They are to work harder than anybody else. And then, because the world is looking for a hero, they introduce Jesus to these people who are lost and dying. God is building His people to become the instruments that He can use—to be the distributors of His goodness and goods upon the face of the earth.[47]

---

[47] Pastor Tim Cobrae, interview by Tony Cooke. http://www.rockchurch.com/resources/details/rev._tony_cooke_interview

Someone who has been able to implement this approach is Gary from the St. Louis area. Gary delivers meals to patients at a Catholic hospital. Of his "job," he shares the following:

> With each tray, we also give a comment card, and I always write my name on it along with the message, "God bless you." I often have an opportunity to pray with patients, and that is a great joy to me because I know some of them are lonely, afraid, and hurting. If it seems that a person is receptive, I will tell them "You know, I pray for all of my patients." Many times they will say, "Really? That's great," and that's when I will ask them if they would like for me to pray with them. Many people take me up on the offer. Whether they ask for prayer or not, I never leave the room without telling them, "God bless you," and, "Have a blessed day!"
>
> My job is delivering food trays, but I see myself as the Lord's ambassador, delivering spiritual nourishment and letting patients know that someone cares about them. I am honored to be used of God in this manner, and I take my responsibility very seriously. I typically serve around 40–50 patients a day; for the last few years, I have passed at least 8,000 trays or more. In 2013, I received the Exceptional Employee Award for patient care. I always strive to not just do the minimum required, but to also go above and beyond, ensuring my patient's needs are always met.

Gary's actions on the job speak to his awareness of God's purpose for his life. He doesn't neglect his job duties by preaching to patients, and he doesn't cross the line between respect for the patient and the call to be a godly witness. Rather, he does his job with excellence and then finds ways to show the love and light of Christ whenever and wherever he can.

Some might say, "But I have a job where witnessing is against the company policy, so I really can't say 'God bless you,' pray for people, or tell others about Jesus where I work." That is something many employees encounter, but that doesn't mean we can't set a great example as believers and still be witnesses (as opposed to active witnessing). After all, no company has rules against working hard, having a positive attitude, being courteous and kind to others, and being a grateful, respectful person.

Others find themselves in job settings where those around them don't share their godly values. A believer may be surrounded by foul language, ungodly stories, and atrocious attitudes, yet he has an opportunity to let his lifestyle be a good witness. A worker in this type of situation should ask himself, *Is my lifestyle, my attitude, my character, and the "fruit" of my life while I'm on the clock sufficient to generate questions from others when I'm off the clock?*

Believers in Peter's day lived and worked in what was often a hostile environment, and he counseled them, "[Have] your conduct honorable among the Gentiles, that when they speak against you as evildoers, they may, by your good works which they observe, glorify God in the day of visitation" (1 Peter 2:12). Peter proceeded to say, "But even if you suffer for doing what is right, God will reward you for it. So don't worry or be afraid of their threats. Instead, you must worship Christ as Lord of your life. And if someone asks about your Christian hope, always be ready to explain it" (1 Peter 3:14–15, *NLT*).

Paul's instructions to Christians coincides well with what Peter said: "Walk in wisdom toward those who are outside, redeeming the time. Let your speech always be with grace, seasoned with salt, that you may know how you ought to answer each one" (Colossians 4:5–6).

The Bible instructs us about *why* we work (for the glory of God), but it also teaches us *how* to work. We have the responsibility and privilege of being diligent workers who serve as unto the Lord, living respectable lives, prospering, and giving generously to others. Our work ethic can testify of what God has done in our lives and be a witness to others of God's goodness and love.

Quotes Worth Remembering

"The average person puts only 25% of his energy and ability into his work. The world takes off its hat to those who put in more than 50% of their capacity, and stands on its head for those few and far between souls who devote 100%."
—Andrew Carnegie

"There may be people who have more talent than you, but there's no excuse for anyone to work harder than you do—and I believe that."
—Derek Jeter

"I am wondering what would have happened to me if some fluent talker had converted me to the theory of the eight-hour day and convinced me that it was not fair to my fellow workers to put forth my best efforts in my work. I am glad that the eight-hour work day had not been invented when I was a young man. If my life had been made up of eight-hour days I do not believe I could have accomplished a great deal. This country would not amount to as much as it does if the young men of fifty years ago had been afraid that they might earn more money than they were paid."
—Thomas Edison

"Always do more than is required of you."
—John Wooden

"Football teaches you hard work. It takes a lot of unspectacular preparation to have spectacular results in both business and football."
—Roger Staubach

Questions for Reflection and Discussion

1. Think through the story of *The Little Red Hen*. What is your reaction when you read this? Can you relate to this story in one way or another?

2. Review the list of scriptures in Proverbs about work and laziness. Have you seen any of those principles (positive or negative) at work in your own life?

3. In your past and current experience, what kind of work ethic have you seen displayed by people around you? What kinds of attitudes toward work have you seen in others? Are people typically punctual or late? Do people tend to have a good attitude, or do they grumble and complain a lot? Do people tend to give their best effort, or do they tend to do just enough to get by?

4. Paul set a very high standard for the Colossians' attitude toward and diligence in their work. He told them, "Do your best. Work from the heart for your real Master, for God. . . . Keep in mind always that the ultimate Master you're serving is Christ" (Colossians 3:22–24, *MSG*). To what degree has this ideal has been integrated into your attitude and implemented in your work habits?

5. Review Pastor Jim Cobrae's comments. Have there been times in your life when you lived out this concept? Have you been able to be a light and a positive example to others in your place of work?

REFLECTIONS FROM READERS

Chuck from Pennsylvania writes:

I can remember myself as a child, watching my father go off to work day in and day out and never complaining about the weather or how difficult his job was. He was a steel mill worker and worked for 40 years to provide a stable environment for our family. My father instilled a good work ethic in each of us. When I was 15 years old, I wanted to get a job so that I could have extra money, so I began going from store to store, asking if anyone was in need of help. My first job was washing windows at a local cleaners. I didn't want to disappoint my father by having someone report to him that I didn't do a good job, so I made those windows shine. They gave me a good reference to a local laundry where I began pressing shirts.

I made it a point to always go beyond what my employer asked of me. My jobs were not glamorous, but I did whatever my hand found to do with all that I had inside of me. When I left one employer to go to a different job, I never had to worry about what my previous boss might say. Even the people who worked for me knew that I would never ask them to do something that I would not be willing to do myself. I was just as happy cleaning toilets as I was sitting in the CEO chair, and my attitude toward the job was always the same: work as if you are working for God, and you will be blessed beyond measure.

Scott from Nebraska writes:

Both of my parents worked; my father worked in construction, my mother in office administration. A large part of my

REFLECTIONS FROM READERS

parents' motivation to work was their love for their children and their determination to provide my brother and me all that we needed to get a good start in life. They also did all the things necessary to raise and take care of my brother and me, so I had good role models of people who worked diligently and took pride in their accomplishments and the results of their efforts.

Two scriptures have influenced my attitude towards my job and my ability to earn a living in this world's system:

❖ The first is a paraphrase of Psalm 75:6–7: "Don't exalt yourself, for promotion comes from the Lord."

❖ The second is Colossians 3:23–24, which says, "Work as unto the Lord . . . as it is Christ you are serving."

Several promotions and career changes arose as I identified positions that I desired, even though the jobs seemed unreachable to me at the time. In those cases, I reflected on the example of David, who tended sheep, not knowing that he was being prepared to lead a nation of God's people. I decided that a proper response to a "closed door" would be to apply myself with all diligence to my current job, continually working "as unto Christ."

In retrospect, those times when the work was tedious and the rewards vague, my continuing to apply full concentration and effort allowed me to keep a positive attitude, and this has always resulted in moving to a better place in God's blessing.

REFLECTIONS FROM READERS

It is clear now that all the promotions and new opportunities were from the Lord.

Paula from Illinois writes:

The mission of the health care organization I work for is "to serve persons with the greatest care and love," which is a strong motivator for me. This mission aligns nicely with my own personal values. My father taught me at a very early age that the more you give to life and put into it, the more you will get out of it. I am motivated by inspiring employees to rally around this common mission of service and by seeing the impact that we have on personal lives and on the overall well-being of the community. Developing people and seeing them be successful are great thrills for me. I am also motivated by being a role model to my two children.

Beth from Oklahoma writes:

I am thankful I grew up with parents who trained me to work. They displayed consistent hard work themselves.

My three realms of work are my home, my church, and my job. Although only my job pays me for working, I don't work harder at my job than I do in the home or at church. Regardless of where I am, I try to always be conscious that God sees me and what I do. I especially think of this when I pick up trash outside or when I wash coffee cups that co-workers left in the sink for the "magic fairy." I do my work as unto the Lord and to humble myself. Similarly, I work in my local church as

REFLECTIONS FROM READERS

a means of serving the Lord, having learned the principle that while I am in my church to receive, I am also there to give.

Another gentleman God has used tremendously to support his church and other ministries shares his story:

My journey has included ups and downs, dark moments and bright spots, but in recent years, God has put me on a very positive and productive track. I was raised in church but fell away from God and church in college. I started practicing law in the early 1970s, but because God was not a part of my life, my perspective and mindset were off base.

I was 23 when I started practicing law and by 26, I was a young criminal prosecutor being driven by ego. I enjoyed the prestige and the thrill of power—deciding who to prosecute and who not to prosecute. My end game was political. I was going to climb the ladder, and I was determined to win at any cost. I was taken aback after one trial when a juror told me, "You had so much hate in your eyes." Needless to say, there were no Christian motives operating in my life at all.

For several years, I practiced eastern religions but never found fulfillment in them. Thankfully, God sent a powerful soul-winner across my path, someone who dynamically affected my life. Little did I know at that time all that God had in store for the future. I got involved in an independent, Spirit-filled church, and it wasn't long before I began practicing the biblical principle of tithing.

REFLECTIONS FROM READERS

Around the time I started tithing, I began recognizing that my steps had been ordered by heaven even when I wasn't walking with God. I saw that He was the One who had given me the skills and abilities I had, and that I was to use them for His glory and for the building and advancement of His kingdom. Some time after this, my wife and I felt that God was leading me to step away from practicing law and that we were to begin a new company that focused on investing. My business partner and I determined that all our work would be for the glory of God.

At one point, we needed a major breakthrough. For a year-and-a-half, my wife and I both had it on our hearts to help a couple in our church to get into a nice house. After we did that, things broke loose, and we have experienced tremendous blessings in our life and business since that time (though not without obstacles).

When our church had some major projects, we felt challenged by God to respond and help in a major way. In almost all cases, we did not know how we would accomplish what God was directing us to do, but we learned to step out in faith and trust God for his promises. We seldom had the material resources at the moment, but we understood that God had called us and given us a purpose to be Kingdom benefactors. God came through for us, and we came through for the church. One year, we actually gave more to the church than we made ourselves. Of course, we had reserves to draw from, but we believe this is why God has blessed us so much. My wife and I will never have a billion dollars because we will have given it away before we could accumulate that much. God does not want us to be a bottleneck; rather, He wants us to be distributors of His blessings.

I used to worship money; I chased it; and I failed every time. Money is only a means to an end. It is a tool, and it has to be used according to God's plan. God is the One who has given us the wisdom to do things that others have not been able to do. People get hung up on worshipping money and worshipping things, but that's not what our lives are about. I recognize that money is needed to live and do what we do, but money is not my goal in life, and it is certainly not my god. I aspire to glorify God, to fund the Gospel, and to do my job well.

Further, we want to represent God to people. Various workers who have come to our home have asked us questions that have enabled us to witness and share our faith with them. We have been able to encourage them to go to church, and we have seen their lives changed. Occasionally, we host dinners at a local club that is frequented by wealthy people, and both management and staff have thanked us for our conduct. They have told us how pleasant it is for them to host an event like ours where there is no cussing or drinking and where the workers are treated with kindness, dignity, and respect.

REFLECTIONS FROM READERS

Our lives have been mightily influenced by God's love, and it is our desire to allow God's love to influence others through us. Whether it is through our work, our giving, or our character, we are here to glorify God with all that we have and all that we are. That is our purpose, and that is what brings fulfillment to our lives.

CHAPTER FIVE

Works that Glorify God Beyond the Workplace: Volunteerism and Labors of Love

"He who thinks that he is being released from the work, and not set free in order that he may accomplish that work, mistakes the Christ from whom the freedom comes, mistakes the condition into which his soul is invited."
—Phillips Brooks

In his book *The Volunteer Revolution*, Pastor Bill Hybels speaks of the kinds of works that transcend people's employment:

It's as if God has work gloves on. And he calls us to roll up our sleeves and join him with our talents, our money, our time, and our passion. He wants his mission to become ours.... The desire to be a world-changer is planted in the heart of every human being, and that desire comes directly from the heart of God. We can suffocate that desire in selfishness, silence it with the chatter of competing demands, or bypass it on the fast track to personal achievement, but it's still there. Whenever we wonder if the daily eight-to-five grind or our round-the-clock parenting tasks are all there is to life, that divine desire nudges us. Whenever we feel restless and unsatisfied, the desire whispers in our soul. Whenever we wonder what a life of real purpose would feel like, the desire calls us to something more.[48]

This "something more" involves acts of service, whether they be done on the job or off the clock. These acts of service, or "good works," aren't something we do to earn a paycheck; they aren't part of the job description. These are the deeds that God inspires and calls us to perform—for His glory and for the benefit of others.

In the last two chapters, I dealt primarily with work that fits within the scope of employment, but this chapter addresses those works that transcend (go above and beyond) employment issues. We are called to apply our time, our energy, and our efforts to far more than just our jobs.

What about applying our efforts to building meaningful relationships with our family? Applying effort toward cultivating wholeness and growth in our own life, and greater depth in our relationship with God? Applying effort toward serving and blessing others?

We are here to make a difference in the world, and change happens when people act. What immediately follows the four Gospels is the Book of *Acts*, not the Book of *Meditations* (emphasis mine). Actions are important! Early in His ministry, Jesus made it clear to His disciples that they were called to produce good works, saying, "Let your light so shine before men, that they may see your good works and glorify your Father in heaven" (Matthew 5:16).

---

[48] Hybels, Bill. *The Volunteer Revolution* (Grand Rapids, Michigan: Zondervan, 2004), 13–14.

What Kind of Good Works Did Jesus Commend?

During His earthly ministry, Jesus did not take a passive, oblivious perspective of the good works people did. Instead, He recognized and extolled peoples' efforts when they did commendable things. For example:

❖ Jesus said that a person who gave "even a cup of cold water to one of the least of [His] followers . . . will surely be rewarded" (Matthew 10:42, *NLT*).

❖ Jesus commended those who gave food and drink to the hungry and thirsty, who gave lodging to the stranger, who clothed the naked, and who visited the sick and the imprisoned (Matthew 25:35–36).

❖ Of the woman who anointed Him with oil in Bethany, Jesus said that she had done "a good work" and stated that " wherever this gospel is preached in the whole world, what this woman has done will also be told as a memorial to her" (Matthew 26:10, 13).

❖ Jesus spoke positively of the Samaritan who had compassion on the wounded man, bandaged his wounds, poured in the oil and wine, and arranged for his lodging while he recovered (Luke 10:30–37).

❖ Jesus lauded the sacrificial generosity of the widow who gave her last two coins at the temple (Luke 21:1–4).

Not only do our good works benefit others, but they also matter to Jesus. And if they matter to Jesus, they matter to His Father.

What Jesus Taught About Our Works

After Jesus fed the multitudes, he had an interesting interaction with some of the people who been recipients of His miraculous work.

JOHN 6:27–29

27 "Do not labor for the food which perishes, but for the food which endures to everlasting life, which the Son of Man will give you, because God the Father has set His seal on Him."
28 Then they said to Him, "What shall we do, that we may work the works of God?"
29 Jesus answered and said to them, "This is the work of God, that you believe in Him whom He sent."

Jesus was not saying that it's wrong to work for wages which are then used to provide for one's needs. He was saying that we must have a higher purpose than mere survival, a purpose that goes beyond meeting our rudimentary needs. Jesus taught that our works—whatever we do in this life—must be faith-based. An accurate perception of who Jesus is and our belief in Him should be at the core of and the impetus for everything we do in life.

The New American Commentary explains this passage from John in this way:

Acceptability with God cannot be on the basis of "belief" in a mere theological formulation about God. Thus the noun "faith" (*pistis*) does not occur in John's Gospel. He chose instead to use only the verb "believe" (*pisteuein*), and he almost equated it with "obey." Acceptability with God is a relationship God gives, therefore, and both believing and obeying are parallel ways one acknowledges dependence on God. As the Son always responded appropriately to the Father, people are to respond to the Son, who was sent by the Father. That is precisely the way John understood the call of Jesus to the Jews here.[49]

There is a human tendency to want to work our way into acceptance by God. A believing heart, though, is the response God desires from us. When we believe Him, the actions that flow from our lives can be faith-based, not some kind of frantic, despairing attempt to earn God's favor. What we do needs to flow from what Jesus described when He said, "I am the vine, you are the branches. He who abides in Me, and I in him, bears much fruit; for without Me you can do nothing" (John 15:5). When we are connected to the Vine, we should bear much fruit, and this "fruit" is not our path to salvation but the byproduct of salvation; this "fruit" is our good works.

While Jesus taught that faith, or believing, is the foundation for our relationship with God, it is also important to understand that true biblical believing is not mere mental assent. Rather, biblical believing can be seen in the outward actions that follow. We see works springing from belief in another statement that Jesus made: "Most assuredly, I say to you, he who believes in Me, the works that I do he will do also; and greater works than these he will do, because I go to My Father" (John 14:12).

There have been many discussions and debates over what Jesus meant when He said that we would not only do the works He did, but that we would do even greater works. After all, how could we do greater works than walking on water or raising the dead? How do we do greater works than cleansing the lepers and making the lame to walk? That sounds like a pretty tall order. Perhaps we've missed great opportunities related to John 14:12 because we've assumed that "greater works" meant more dramatic,

---

[49] Borchert, Gerald L. John 1–11. *The New American Commentary* (Nashville: Broadman & Holman Publishers, 1996).

more spectacular, and more sensational. Perhaps we should ponder what Jesus would consider "greater works." The Lord said, "Whoever desires to become great among you, let him be your servant" (Matthew 20:26). If I understand this properly, we will see the same and greater works expressed when we focus on serving extravagantly, which is how Jesus defined greatness.

I believe that a key to understanding the greater works involves the phrase "because I go to the Father." Elsewhere, Jesus taught that when He went to the Father, the Holy Spirit would then be sent to indwell and empower believers (John 7:39; 16:7; Luke 24:49; Acts 1:8). Because Jesus' representatives were anointed by the Spirit, they were able to do the kinds of works Jesus did, and even greater works, just as Jesus said.

In what way were their works "greater" than those of Jesus?

1. Their works were greater *geographically*. Jesus ministered in the relatively small confines of Israel, whereas His early disciples travelled throughout the Roman Empire and beyond.

2. Their works were greater *numerically*. Jesus' personal ministry, during His time on earth, was limited to people with whom He could interact within the limitations of His own physical body. He could only be in one place at one time. However, as the early believers were empowered by the Spirit, Jesus' ministry was no longer limited to one person, and God was able to minister to many more people because there were now many Spirit-empowered believers through whom He could minister.

3. Their works were greater *spiritually*. Some might balk at this and think that nothing could be more spiritual than

Jesus' ministry. But keep in mind, when Jesus was here on earth, the Spirit had not been given the way He would be after Jesus' resurrection. After the resurrection, people could actually become born-again and Spirit-filled in a way that was not possible before. Hence, the early disciples had the distinct privilege of leading people into the New Birth and into the infilling of the Holy Spirit—something Jesus did not personally do while ministering on earth.

4. Their works were greater *in scope*. Jesus' ministry was primarily geared toward teaching, preaching, and healing; while the early disciples continued those works, they also began to build fully-constituted New Testament congregations. Even in the miraculous realm, there were types of healings that took place in the early Church that had not occurred in Jesus' ministry. People were healed when Peter's shadow passed over them (Acts 5:15–16) and also when cloths were taken to the sick from the Apostle Paul (Acts 19:11–12). In natural areas, disciples in later generations would build and operate orphanages, schools, homeless shelters, and hospitals in Jesus' name. Publishing houses would print and distribute Bibles and Christian literature; radio and television stations would broadcast the Gospel to mass multitudes. Satellite and Internet technology now convey God's Word to every corner of the world. Evangelists and missionaries conduct mass evangelistic and healing meetings and reach millions of lost and hurting people with the message and power of God's love.

Jesus was very serious when He said that we would do the works He did, and even greater works. If we truly believe and obey Him, we will set our hearts to do just that. The early disciples picked up the torch and began doing His works and the greater works, and it is our responsibility to continue doing the same today.

Not Just *What*, but *How* and *Why*

The Lord isn't concerned just with *what* works we do, but also with *how* and *why* we do them. *How* we work (the attitude we have while working) and *why* we work (our motive and the intent of our heart) are just as important as the outward result, because God looks on the heart. We see this vividly illustrated in the Book of Acts. Joses (Barnabas) was a good-hearted and sincere man. He sold some property and laid it at the feet of the apostles. Ananias and Saphira imitated the actions of Barnabas, but their hearts were deceptive, and while Barnabas was honored, Ananias and Saphira were struck dead (Acts 4:36–5:10). In Matthew 6:1–18, we learn that we are not to give charitably, pray, or fast in order to receive recognition or accolades from men. We do what we do to honor God as though no one were watching. In each of these situations (giving, praying, and fasting), Jesus said, "And your Father who sees in secret will Himself reward you openly" (Matthew 6:4, 6, 18).

What can we learn from these passages? Not everything that looks like a good work is in fact a good work. Indeed, one of Jesus' harshest indictments was directed at people who claimed to have done many good works, and yet engaged in wickedness.

MATTHEW 7:21–23

21 "Not everyone who says to Me, 'Lord, Lord,' shall enter the kingdom of heaven, but he who does the will of My Father in heaven.

22 Many will say to Me in that day, 'Lord, Lord, have we not prophesied in Your name, cast out demons in Your name, and done many wonders in Your name?'

23 And then I will declare to them, 'I never knew you; depart from Me, you who practice lawlessness!'"

Doing the will of God from the heart is at the core of all that the New Testament teaches. Our *actions* might say one thing; but God sees our heart and knows what our *motives* are saying.

The Apostle Paul on Good Works

The Apostle Paul has long been known as the Apostle of Grace, and rightly so. He was adamant in his teaching that we are not saved by works (Acts 2:8–9; Titus 3:3–7), and yet he was a powerful proponent of believers engaging in good works. Paul did not want believers working in some misguided attempt to earn their salvation, but rather, he wanted them to work in order to express their salvation—to glorify God and benefit others.

Some people mistakenly believe that faith and works (or grace and works) are somehow antithetical. I suppose they could be if a person were trying to work for something that God has freely given, something that is only to be received by faith and not by works. But in another sense, our works (our corresponding actions) can complement and express our faith. For example, when Paul told Agrippa about his ministry, he said that he had "declared first to those in Damascus and in Jerusalem, and throughout all the region of Judea, and then to the Gentiles, that they should repent, turn to God, and *do works befitting repentance*" (Acts 26:20, emphasis mine).

As one reads through Paul's epistles, it's difficult to read very far without seeing his strong admonitions for believers to be workers and to serve others in love. The list is extensive:

- ❖ "Therefore, my beloved brethren, be steadfast, immovable, always abounding in the work of the Lord, knowing that your labor is not in vain in the Lord" (1 Corinthians 15:58).

- ❖ "And God is able to make all grace abound toward you, that you, always having all sufficiency in all things, may have an abundance for every good work" (2 Corinthians 9:8).

- ❖ "Pay careful attention to your own work, for then you will get the satisfaction of a job well done, and you won't need to compare yourself to anyone else" (Galatians 6:4, *NLT*).

- ❖ "For we are God's masterpiece. He has created us anew in Christ Jesus, so we can do the good things he planned for us long ago" (Ephesians 2:10, *NLT*).

According to Paul, we have a lot of work to do—good works, that flow from our salvation and relationship with God.

In Ephesians chapter 4, Paul lists different types of preachers, and then tells us the purpose for which those ministers were given. We read, "Now these are the gifts Christ gave to the church: the apostles, the prophets, the evangelists, and the pastors and teachers. Their responsibility is to equip God's people to do his work and build up the church, the body of Christ" (Ephesians 4:11-12, *NLT*). Isn't it interesting—preachers aren't called to do all the work themselves, but "to equip God's people to do [His] work." A few short verses later, Paul makes it clear that all of God's children are to be workers—that each and every believer has a vital contribution to make. Speaking of Christ as the Head of the Church, Paul said, "He makes the whole body fit together perfectly. As each part does its own special work, it helps the other parts grow, so that the whole body is healthy and growing and full of love" (Ephesians 4:16, *NLT*).

Paul's compendium of thought on the subject of work continues:

❖ "Therefore, my beloved, as you have always obeyed, not as in my presence only, but now much more in my absence, work out your own salvation with fear and trembling" (Philippians 2:12).

❖ " . . . that you may walk worthy of the Lord, fully pleasing Him, being fruitful in every good work and increasing in the knowledge of God" (Colossians 1:10).

❖ ". . . remembering without ceasing your work of faith, labor of love, and patience of hope in our Lord Jesus Christ in the sight of our God and Father" (1 Thessalonians 1:3).

❖ "May he give you the power to accomplish all the good things your faith prompts you to do" (2 Thessalonians 1:11, *NLT*).

❖ "Now may our Lord Jesus Christ Himself, and our God and Father . . . comfort your hearts and establish you in every good word and work" (2 Thessalonians 2:16–17).

❖ "Good works are also obvious, and the ones that are not cannot remain hidden" (1 Timothy 5:25, *NET*).

❖ Paul gave certain qualifications for elderly widows to be eligible to receive support from the church. A widow being considered for support must have had a history of well-reported good works, including that of lodging strangers, washing the feet of other believers, and relieving the afflicted; in other words, she had to be known for "diligently follow[ing] every good work" (1 Timothy 5:10).

❖ Concerning those wealthy in this world, Paul said, "Tell them to use their money to do good. They should be rich in good works and generous to those in need, always being ready to share with others" (1 Timothy 6:18, *NLT*).

❖ If Paul is the author of Hebrews, he also said, "For God is not unjust to forget your work and labor of love which you have shown toward His name, in that you have ministered to the saints, and do minister" (Hebrews 6:10).

❖ The promotion of good works was to be a joint project among believers. Hebrews 10:24 says, "And let us consider one another in order to stir up love and good works."

❖ At the end of Hebrews, we read a strongly expressed desire that God would "make you complete in every good work to do His will, working in you what is well pleasing in His sight" (Hebrews 13:21).

Paul, the Apostle of Grace, says quite a bit about works, proving that faith and works (and grace and works) are not at odds but work together in the plan of God.

Titus: The Book of Good Works

When I was taking a New Testament Survey Course in Bible school, I was introduced to the Book of Titus and was told that it was sometimes referred to as "The Book of Good Works." Paul had left Titus, one of his young associate ministers, on the island of Crete in the Mediterranean Sea so that Titus could "set in order the things that are lacking, and appoint elders in every city" (Titus 1:5). Before we look at the important passages in the Book of Titus that pertain to good works, it would be helpful if we first look at the people in Titus' care. The inhabitants of this island had an unsavory reputation, and Paul pulled no punches in describing the reality that existed behind their notoriety.

TITUS 1:10–13 (*NLT*)

10 For there are many rebellious people who engage in useless talk and deceive others. This is especially true of those who insist on circumcision for salvation.

11 They must be silenced, because they are turning whole families away from the truth by their false teaching. And they do it only for money.

12 Even one of their own men, a prophet from Crete, has said about them, "The people of Crete are all liars, cruel animals, and lazy gluttons."

13 This is true. So reprimand them sternly to make them strong in the faith.

Paul went on to describe some of these individuals: "They profess to know God, but in works they deny Him, being abominable, disobedient, and disqualified for every good work" (Titus 1:16). That's quite a sobering description. Paul understood that what people *say* isn't always the ultimate indicator of what's inside; it's what people *do* that really defines them. Proverbs 20:11 says, "Even a child is known by his deeds, whether what he does is pure and right." It was along these lines that Thomas Jefferson said, "Do you want to know who you are? Don't ask. Act! Action will delineate and define you."

William Barclay wrote, "The Cretans were famed as a drunken, insolent, untrustworthy, lying, gluttonous people." He proceeded to say, "So notorious were the Cretans that the Greeks actually formed a verb *krētizein*, to cretize, which meant to lie and to cheat; and they had a proverbial phrase, *krētizein pros Krēta*, to cretize against a Cretan, which meant to match lies with lies, as diamond cuts diamond." Barclay further explained:

> The Cretans were notorious liars and cheats and gluttons and traitors but here is the wonderful thing. Knowing that, and actually experiencing it, Paul does not say to Timothy: "Leave them alone. They are hopeless and all men know it." He says: "They are bad and all men know it. Go and convert them." Few passages so demonstrate the divine optimism of the Christian evangelist, who refuses to regard any man as hopeless. The greater the evil, the greater the challenge. It is the Christian conviction that there is no sin too great for the grace of Jesus Christ to conquer.[50]

Were these very unflattering descriptions true of every citizen in Crete? Certainly not, but it seems that there were enough instances to lend credibility to the stereotypes which existed. Some scholars believe, and perhaps rightly so, that Paul's harshest remarks were specifically targeted toward the false teachers in Crete, not toward the population as a whole.

It seems clear that Paul did not mean to paint everyone in Crete with the same brush, since he told Titus to select men of virtuous character— Cretan men—for leadership positions in the church (Titus 1:5–9). If no believers on the island possessed good character traits at all, Paul would not have given Titus this assignment. One commentary notes, "Of course many noble Christians were in the congregations in Crete, but Paul was frontal in his assertion that the false teachers possessed these baser Cretan tendencies."[51]

---

[50] Barclay, William, editor. *The Letters to Timothy, Titus, and Philemon: The Daily Study Bible Series* (Philadelphia: Westminster John Knox Press, 1975).
[51] Walvoord, John F., Roy B. Zuck and Dallas Theological Seminary. *The Bible Knowledge Commentary: An Exposition of the Scriptures* (Wheaton, IL: Victor Books, 1985).

How would you like to be given the assignment of ministering on that island? Titus was not given an assignment to go where there was a predominantly Christian population. Most people in Titus' sphere of influence were not sophisticated, refined, gentle souls.

So How Were These Problems Addressed?

Suffice it to say that there were a good number of people on the island of Crete who had been negatively affected, to one degree or another, by the indigenous and deeply ingrained cultural tendencies. So what did Paul tell Titus to do to address these issues? How was this young minister going to lead believers in Crete into more godly character and behavior? Paul's admonitions to Titus make it very clear that Paul wanted the influence of Truth to create an honest, solid work ethic in their lives:

- ❖ "In all things showing yourself to be a pattern of good works; in doctrine showing integrity, reverence, incorruptibility" (Titus 2:7).

- ❖ "...who gave Himself for us, that He might redeem us from every lawless deed and purify for Himself His own special people, zealous for good works" (Titus 2:14).

- ❖ "Remind them to be subject to rulers and authorities, to obey, to be ready for every good work" (Titus 3:1).

- ❖ "This is a faithful saying, and these things I want you to affirm constantly, that those who have believed in God should be careful to maintain good works. These things are good and profitable to men" (Titus 3:8).

- ❖ "And let our people also learn to maintain good works, to meet urgent needs, that they may not be unfruitful" (Titus 3:14).

Titus is a relatively short book in the New Testament, but the need for the people of Crete to develop a solid work ethic must have been extremely important for Paul to have emphasized good works the way he did.

James and Good Works

James, the Lord's brother (half-brother, to be technically correct) became a significant leader in the church in Jerusalem. As he watched Christianity grow in its first decades, James became alarmed that some people were substituting dead orthodoxy for a living relationship that evinces belief in Christ. (In other words, people had the right "beliefs," but they had no fruit or corresponding actions that proceeded from those beliefs.) He wrote to the believers there in powerful terms, admonishing them that works were an integral part of true faith. I appreciate the way *The Message* renders his words:

JAMES 2:14–26
14 Dear friends, do you think you'll get anywhere in this if you learn all the right words but never do anything? Does merely talking about faith indicate that a person really has it?
15 For instance, you come upon an old friend dressed in rags and half-starved
16 and say, "Good morning, friend! Be clothed in Christ! Be filled with the Holy Spirit!" and walk off without providing so much as a coat or a cup of soup—where does that get you?
17 Isn't it obvious that God-talk without God-acts is outrageous nonsense?

18 I can already hear one of you agreeing by saying, "Sounds good. You take care of the faith department, I'll handle the works department." Not so fast. You can no more show me your

works apart from your faith than I can show you my faith apart from my works. Faith and works, works and faith, fit together hand in glove.

19 Do I hear you professing to believe in the one and only God, but then observe you complacently sitting back as if you had done something wonderful? That's just great. Demons do that, but what good does it do them?

20 Use your heads! Do you suppose for a minute that you can cut faith and works in two and not end up with a corpse on your hands?

21 Wasn't our ancestor Abraham "made right with God by works" when he placed his son Isaac on the sacrificial altar?

22 Isn't it obvious that faith and works are yoked partners, that faith expresses itself in works? That the works are "works of faith"?

23 The full meaning of "believe" in the Scripture sentence, "Abraham believed God and was set right with God," includes his action. It's that mesh of believing and acting that got Abraham named "God's friend."

24 Is it not evident that a person is made right with God not by a barren faith but by faith fruitful in works?

25 The same with Rahab, the Jericho harlot. Wasn't her action in hiding God's spies and helping them escape—that seamless unity of believing and doing—what counted with God?

26 The very moment you separate body and spirit, you end up with a corpse. Separate faith and works and you get the same thing: a corpse.

And as if this exposition was not powerful and convincing enough on its own, James followed these amazing remarks with the following two statements:

❖ "But he who looks into the perfect law of liberty and continues in it, and is not a forgetful hearer but a doer of the work, this one will be blessed in what he does" (James 1:25).

❖ "Who is wise and understanding among you? Let him show by good conduct that his works are done in the meekness of wisdom" (James 3:13).

James did not deem the concept of "Fruitless Christianity" to be compatible with God's idea of genuine faith. Mere mental assent—that which intellectually agrees with Christian doctrine, but gives no evidence of Christ-like character or behavior—was not a legitimate expression of true discipleship.

Other Apostolic Witnesses

Peter also addressed the idea of believers doing good works, as did the Apostle John:

❖ "Having your conduct honorable among the Gentiles, that when they speak against you as evildoers, they may, by your good works which they observe, glorify God in the day of visitation" (1 Peter 2:12).

❖ "Dear children, let's not merely say that we love each other; let us show the truth by our actions. Our actions will show that we belong to the truth" (1 John 3:18–19, *NLT*).

Jesus and the Seven Churches

Jesus taught about the importance of good works and commended good works during His earthly ministry, and when he appeared to John on the island of Patmos many years after His resurrection, we see that the works of His people continued to be at the forefront of His thinking. Jesus' emphasis on works was so strong that He said to each of the seven churches, "I know your works."[52] Consider Jesus' communication to each of these local congregations:

❖ To the church in Ephesus: "I know your works, your labor, your patience, and that you cannot bear those who are evil. And you have tested those who say they are apostles and are not, and have found them liars; Remember therefore from where you have fallen; repent and do the first works, or else I will come to you quickly and remove your lampstand from its place—unless you repent" (Revelation 2:2, 5).

❖ To the church in Smyrna: "I know your works, tribulation, and poverty (but you are rich); and I know the blasphemy of those who say they are Jews and are not, but are a synagogue of Satan" (Revelation 2:9).

❖ To the church in Pergamum: "I know your works, and where you dwell, where Satan's throne is. And you hold fast to My name, and did not deny My faith even in the days in which Antipas was My faithful martyr, who was killed among you, where Satan dwells" (Revelation 2:13).

❖ To the church in Thyatira: "I know your works, love, service, faith, and your patience; and as for your works, the last are more than the first. . . . And I will give to each one of you according to your works. . . . And he who overcomes, and keeps My

---

[52] Observant students may notice in particular modern translations (those based on earlier Greek manuscripts) that Jesus' reference to works is absent in His remarks to the churches of Smyrna and Pergamum. If those earlier manuscripts are the more accurate, this omission is most likely due to the fact that those two churches were encountering significant persecution at that time. It seems reasonable that Jesus, while He is interested in the works of believers, chose not to deal with the issue of works in the light of their distress.

works until the end, to him I will give power over the nations" (Revelation 2:19, 23, 26).

❖ To the church in Sardis: "I know your works, that you have a name that you are alive, but you are dead. Be watchful, and strengthen the things which remain, that are ready to die, for I have not found your works perfect before God" (Revelation 3:1–2).

❖ To the church in Philadelphia: "I know your works. See, I have set before you an open door, and no one can shut it; for you have a little strength, have kept My word, and have not denied My name" (Revelation 3:8).

❖ To the church in Laodicea: "I know your works, that you are neither cold nor hot. I could wish you were cold or hot" (Revelation 3:15).

We know that Jesus is the same yesterday, today, and forever (Hebrews 13:8). Therefore, if Jesus was vitally concerned about the works of believers and churches in John's day, He is still vitally concerned about the works of believers today.

If we've somehow allowed our love for the Lord and others to diminish (as had happened in Ephesus), Jesus wants us to do the first works—the types of works we did when we were passionately in love with the Lord. If our works are incomplete as they were in Sardis, He wants us to fully carry out the work we've been called to do on heaven's behalf.

The Value of Volunteers

I believe with all of my heart that we are going to see an army of workers arise—men, women, and young people—whose hearts God has called to serve Him. May we revisit the reality of Psalm 110:3, which says, "Your people will volunteer freely in the day of Your power" (*NASB*). One commentary says the literal meaning of this verse is, "Thy people are free will offerings."[53] Another says the word "volunteer" refers to "an entirely cheerful readiness" and says that the Messiah's people will be "ready for any sacrifices, they bring themselves with all that they are and have to meet him. There is no need of any compulsory, lengthy proclamation calling them out: it is no army of mercenaries, but willingly and quickly they present themselves from inward impulse."[54]

It is my heartfelt prayer that we will see a massive uprising of believers who have responded to God's love for humanity and who present themselves as willing and able vessels that God freely and powerfully uses. That will make the difference between the church being a tepid, ineffective, dying institution, and the church being the vibrant, world-changing, life-giving Body that it was intended to be.

---

[53] Jamieson, Robert, A. R. Fausset and David Brown. *Commentary Critical and Explanatory on the Whole Bible* (Oak Harbor, WA: Logos Research Systems, Inc., 1997).
[54] Keil, Carl Friedrich and Franz Delitzsch. *Commentary on the Old Testament* (Peabody, MA: Hendrickson, 1996).

Quotes Worth Remembering

"The miracle is not that we do this work, but that we are happy to do it."
—Mother Teresa

"Life's most persistent and urgent question is: 'What are you doing for others?'"
—Martin Luther King Jr.

"God deserves to be served with all the energy of which we are capable.
If the service of God is worth anything, it is worth everything. We shall find
our best reward in the Lord's work if we do it with determined diligence.
Our labor is not in vain in the Lord, and we know it.
Half-hearted work will bring no reward;
but when we throw our whole soul into the cause,
we shall see prosperity."
—Charles H. Spurgeon

"If the Savior could die for the world, can't we work for it?"
—D.L. Moody

"The kingdom of God does not consist in talk, but in power, that is, in works
and practice. God loves the 'doers of the word' in faith and love,
and not the 'mere hearers,' who, like parrots,
have learned to utter certain expressions with readiness."
—Martin Luther

Questions for Reflection and Discussion

1. Bill Hybels teaches that there are people who don't receive ultimate fulfillment out of their regular jobs, but find greater or additional satisfaction through volunteering. How much fulfillment do you receive out of your regular job and your volunteering respectively?

2. How do you personally process what Jesus said about our doing the works that He did and even greater works? Does that inspire you, challenge you, or intimidate you? How can that promise be more fully applied and implemented in your own life?

3. If we are not saved by our works, why do you think the Apostle Paul and other Scripture writers placed so much emphasis on believers doing good works?

4. Review James 2:14–26 in *The Message*. Do you feel like you grasp the point James is making? How would you make that same point using your own words?

5. Provide a brief, self-evaluation response to the following "I Want to Serve God, but Where Do I Begin?" questions:

    a. What is my level of spiritual consecration?

    b. How is my servant's attitude?

    c. What is my level of availability?

    d. Am I willing to work?

    e. What am I good at doing?

    f. What are the needs and opportunities around me?

    g. Am I willing to take initiative?

REFLECTIONS FROM READERS

Chilly from Michigan writes:

I've always considered myself an over-achiever. I've had to work harder, study harder, and push harder than many to accomplish the same goals. This is a good thing—in fact, this is a God thing! We're not born extraordinary—no way. We must push past the ordinary with extra effort, passion, and strength to achieve the extraordinary kind of life. We have to continue to work at it in order to live at this level. I believe the work we do should always be the best because "Excellence honors God and reflects His character."

Each morning, I deliberately ask God to "choose *me.*" In other words, if there's a task, an opportunity, or an adventure that requires crazy faith and undaunted determination, I'm in! I'm available! My availability is God's opportunity to do a great work through me.

Work is a natural response to Love. Because I truly love Jesus with all of my heart, soul, mind, and strength, I will work hard to achieve His purposes. Making disciples is hard work; so is being a good husband and father. I'm so thankful for the Holy Spirit's help in knowing exactly how to serve, love, give, listen, and work in a way that is efficient and energy-producing.

Jesus is returning soon. And when He returns, I want to be in the harvest field winning souls, not sitting around in my pajamas with a laptop and cup of tea. Working for the Lord renews my strength! He makes me smile! He keeps me going!

REFLECTIONS FROM READERS

People doing this "work" can do it in such a way that it brings them no attention, pity, or praise. It's a joy! And it glorifies the Lord!

Pam from California writes:

I have always endeavored to ensure that my path is straight, ethical, and honest, and I go out of my way to help people both at work and in my church. I endeavor to give 150% in everything I do and to treat people like God would. I try to anticipate what the next step will be so that I am always ready and not blindsided by something I have forgotten.

I hold several positions at my church. These include leading our greeters and sending cards to people for special events (birthdays, anniversaries, sympathy, new baby, and so forth). I'm also in charge of hospitality (coordinating potlucks and church dinners, and organizing meals for families when needed) and of decorating the church for special events.

I give 150% in my church work for the same reason I give my full effort at my job. Jesus set the example of consistently serving others. How can I not do the same for Him? Life is short, and I believe I need to do all that I can to give my best effort to honor God's love for me.

CHAPTER SIX

The Work of the Ministry: Serving God Is Not for the Lazy

"Now separate to Me Barnabas and Saul for
the work to which I have called them."
—The Holy Spirit (Acts 13:2)

When I was a college student in the late 1970's, some of the guys in our dorm were sitting around talking. Different ones were saying what they planned to do after graduation. One of the students—a business major—said that he was probably going to go into accounting. If that didn't work out, he said, he would probably go into business management. And then he said, with a small chuckle, "And if neither of those work out, I can always go into the ministry." I was shocked! Did he really think that ministry was a profession to arbitrarily enter if other jobs didn't work out? Ministry is a holy calling, not just a fallback plan. Hebrews 5:4 points out that "no man takes this honor to himself, but he who is called by God, just as Aaron was."

Misconceptions regarding ministry abound. Some people think ministry is all spiritual, that ministers spend all their time in prayer or all their time reading the Bible. If you plan on entering the ministry, you'll find that ministry entails doing whatever it takes to get the job done.

Around the time I began writing this book, I saw a social media post by Jeanne Cook. She relayed that her missionary husband, Dennis, was cleaning bat dung out of the radio station attic that they had built in the jungles of Panama. She wrote, "Sometimes you just gotta do what you gotta do. It is not all preaching and teaching on the mission field." Jeanne Cook is so right, and it's not all preaching and teaching anywhere else. Ministry is work. At the end of this chapter, you'll read a dynamic account of the work that the Cooks have engaged in over the years.

Another misconception people have pertains to the workload involved in ministry. Many pastors have been asked, "What is it like to have a job where you only have to work on Sunday?" Such a thought is comical to most pastors, since most of them are expected to be available 24/7. But many people simply don't know the types of challenges involved in leading a congregation. They don't realize that pastors are expected to be at least somewhat knowledgeable, if not highly proficient, in a wide variety of areas, such as the following:

- ❖ Teaching and preaching

- ❖ Prayer

- ❖ Spiritual/biblical counseling

- ❖ Administration of ordinances (baptism and communion)

- ❖ Evangelism

- ❖ Missions

- ❖ Hospital visitation

❖ Conducting funerals and weddings

❖ Christian education

❖ Leadership

❖ Administration

❖ Staff supervision and volunteer management

❖ Marketing and advertising

❖ Conflict management

❖ People skills

❖ Strategic planning

❖ Budgeting

❖ Fund-raising

❖ Public relations and community involvement

❖ Internet technology

❖ Building and facilities management

❖ Audio and video technology

I do not claim that any pastor is perfectly skilled—or even could be—in all of these areas. Pastors, though, still feel a responsibility to minister as effectively as they can, and to make sure that all areas of need are covered in order for the church to be strong within and without.

Blessed are those pastors who recognize their areas of limitations as well as their areas of giftedness and understand the need to delegate. They are truly blessed if they have committed, faithful, and godly people to whom they can delegate. Also, blessed are those believers who recognize that no one individual is gifted or skilled in every given area, who do not put unrealistic expectations on their pastor, and who offer their skills to help fulfill the overall mission of the church.

The New Testament Connection Between Ministry and Work

When Jesus called Peter and Andrew to follow Him, He said, "Follow Me, and I will make you fishers of men" (Matthew 4:19). These two men had long been fishermen by occupation, and they knew by personal experience that fishing was work. From Jesus' teaching (precepts and examples), they would soon learn that ministry was also work. In Matthew chapter 9, Jesus is moved with compassion over the many needs He saw in peoples' lives. He then said to the disciples, "The harvest truly is plentiful, but *the laborers* are few. Therefore pray the Lord of the harvest to send out *laborers* into His harvest" (Matthew 9:37–38, emphasis mine).

Jesus referred to ministry as work again when He sent His disciples out to minister and told them to receive the kindness of others in their travels. He encouraged them to "stay in one place, eating and drinking what they provide. Don't hesitate to accept hospitality, because those who work deserve their pay" (Luke 10:7, *NLT*). You may be more familiar with the way the *King James Version* renders the latter portion of this verse: "The labourer is worthy of his hire."

In John chapter 4, Jesus further describes the ministry assignment of His disciples:

Lift up your eyes and look at the fields, for they are already white for harvest! And he who reaps receives wages, and gathers fruit for eternal life, that both he who sows and he who reaps may rejoice together. For in this the saying is true: "One sows and another reaps." I sent you to reap that for which you have not labored;

others have labored, and you have entered into their labors (John 4:35–38).

As we move into the Book of Acts, the idea of ministry as work continues to be reinforced. Luke's wording makes very clear the work aspect of ministry.

❖ When the Holy Spirit spoke concerning the assignment of Barnabas and Paul, He said, "Now separate to Me Barnabas and Saul for the work to which I have called them" (Acts 13:2).

❖ At the conclusion of that first missionary journey, we read, "Finally, they returned by ship to Antioch of Syria, where their journey had begun. The believers there had entrusted them to the grace of God to do the work they had now completed" (Acts 14:26, *NLT*).

❖ In the middle of that first trip, Mark—whose assignment was to serve Barnabas and Paul—quit and went back to his home in Jerusalem. Later, when it was time for a second missionary journey, Paul's position was "that they should not take with them the one who had departed from them . . . and had not gone with them to the work" (Acts 15:38).

The disciples and the apostles emulated Jesus and obeyed His commands by doing the work of the ministry.

Partnering with God in Ministry Work

Technically, ministry work is not something that we do *for* God. Rather, it is something that we do *with* God. While our labor and involvement are certainly part of the equation, true ministry work is done in partnership with God himself. The best work is done when we are obedient to God and yielded to the Holy Spirit, and He does His work through us.

We catch a glimpse of this in Mark's description of the work of the apostles following the resurrection of Jesus. Mark 16:20 says, "And they went out and preached everywhere, the Lord working with them and confirming the word through the accompanying signs." True New Testament ministry is a joint effort between God's anointing and man's obedience. We are vessels through whom God chooses to work.

Even in the Old Testament, we see a description of collaborative effort between God and man. Following one of Jonathan's exploits, the people said of him, "He has worked with God this day" (1 Samuel 14:45). *The Message* version renders this same statement, "He's been working hand-in-hand with God all day!"

As New Testament believers, we have the distinct advantage of having God living on the inside of us. As we learn to yield to and cooperate with Him, He takes delight in expressing Himself through us. I believe this is why Paul proclaimed, "It is no longer I who live, but Christ lives in me" (Galatians 2:20).

With Christ living in us, it should not seem strange that He would actively energize us and empower us to do what is pleasing to Him and beneficial to others. We see Paul further elaborate on this idea of Christ living and working through us—what we might call a divine partnership—elsewhere in Scripture.

❖ "For we are fellow workmen (joint promoters, laborers together) with and for God" (1 Corinthians 3:9, *AMP*).

❖ In Second Corinthians 6:1, Paul refers to himself and his fellow-ministers as "workers together with [God]." In the *New*

Living Translation of this verse, Paul refers to himself and his fellow ministers as "God's partners."

Isn't this divine partnership a wonderful idea? Not only does God work in us for our benefit, but He also works through us for the benefit of others.

In other places where Paul described his ministerial activities as work, he was also careful to qualify his statements and continue to reference the underlying work of the Holy Spirit which permeated and energized his own efforts:

- ❖ "But by the grace of God I am what I am, and His grace toward me was not in vain; but I labored more abundantly than they all, yet not I, but the grace of God which was with me" (1 Corinthians 15:10).

- ❖ "For this I labor [unto weariness], striving with all the superhuman energy which He so mightily enkindles and works within me" (Colossians 1:29, *AMP*).

While we work, we keep in mind that it is ultimately God's favor and power working through us that makes the difference. As Zechariah 4:6 says, it's "'not by might nor by power, but by My Spirit,' Says the LORD of hosts." This doesn't mean that we don't have to do our part; it means that we recognize that it's ultimately God's power in and through us that is substantive, effective, and influential.

The Work Emphasis Continues

As Paul mentored Timothy, he made sure that his young protégé understood that ministry involves work, and lots of it. Consider these admonitions to his young assistant:

❖ "This is a faithful saying: If a man desires the position of a bishop, he desires a good work" (1 Timothy 3:1).

❖ "Elders who do their work well should be respected and paid well, especially those who work hard at both preaching and teaching" (1 Timothy 5:17, *NLT*).

Paul did not choose soft and delicate metaphors to describe the work of the ministry to Timothy; rather, he used analogies to a soldier, athlete, and farmer, and he emphasized the toughness required in each of these disciplines:

2 TIMOTHY 2:3–6

3 You therefore must endure hardship as a good soldier of Jesus Christ.

4 No one engaged in warfare entangles himself with the affairs of this life, that he may please him who enlisted him as a soldier.

5 And also if anyone competes in athletics, he is not crowned unless he competes according to the rules.

6 The hardworking farmer must be first to partake of the crops.

❖ "Therefore if anyone cleanses himself from the latter, he will be a vessel for honor, sanctified and useful for the Master, prepared for every good work" (2 Timothy 2:21).

❖ After speaking of their inspired nature, Paul tells Timothy that the Scriptures were there so that "the man of God may be complete, thoroughly equipped for every good work" (2 Timothy 3:17).

❖ "But you be watchful in all things, endure afflictions, do the work of an evangelist, fulfill your ministry" (2 Timothy 4:5).

Paul made certain that Timothy knew what ministry would require of him. Paul didn't dilute the amount of energy or effort it would require, and he was very candid with Timothy when detailing the kind of work Timothy would endure during his ministry.

Paul Referred to the Ministry Work of Others

When writing to the Church at Corinth, Paul openly identified himself and Timothy as workers, saying, "And if Timothy comes, see that he may be with you without fear; for he does the work of the Lord, as I also do" (1 Corinthians 16:10). Paul referred to others as workers in subsequent passages:

❖ "I urge you, brethren—you know the household of Stephanas, that it is the firstfruits of Achaia, and that they have devoted themselves to the ministry of the saints—that you also submit to such, and to everyone who works and labors with us" (1 Corinthians 16:15–16).

❖ "Epaphras, who is one of you, a bondservant of Christ, greets you, always laboring fervently for you in prayers, that you may stand perfect and complete in all the will of God" (Colossians 4:12). The Message version renders part of that, "What a trooper he has been! He's been tireless in his prayers for you."

❖ "And we urge you, brethren, to recognize those who labor among you, and are over you in the Lord and admonish you, and to esteem them very highly in love for their work's sake. Be at peace among yourselves" (1 Thessalonians 5:12–13).

125

We can see from Paul's writing that even prayer is referred to as work and that we are to recognize and esteem those who labor among us and on our behalf.

Is It Scriptural to Be Compensated for Ministry?

Like Jesus and Paul, the Apostle John also articulated the work element in his ministry. He told his audience, "Watch out that you do not lose what we have worked so hard to achieve. Be diligent so that you receive your full reward" (2 John 2:8, *NLT*). In addition to referring to ministry as "working so hard," John mentioned an accompanying "reward." Yes, this reward centers on the eternal reward of souls saved for Christ and the divine reward bestowed upon us by our Lord in heaven. But there is also a natural compensation here on earth that needs to be addressed.

Whenever the subject of compensation is brought up, someone usually mentions the fact that Paul labored without monetary reward, choosing instead to work a secular job to meet his personal needs. Lest anyone assume that all pastors should work a secular job for their sole income instead of receiving financial compensation for their ministerial efforts, it is important to understand that Paul taught that he had every right to be compensated for his work. In some situations, Paul personally chose to relinquish that right. Reading the full context of the previous passages makes this principle clear, and Paul dealt with this issue extensively in First Corinthians chapter 9, where he asks the question, "Is it only Barnabas and I who have no right to refrain from working?" (1 Corinthians 9:6).

Paul proceeded to make a powerful argument for all ministers—including himself—to be appropriately compensated for their labors, and then explains why he sometimes forfeits this right:

1 CORINTHIANS 9:12–15 (*NLT*)

12 If you support others who preach to you, shouldn't we have an even greater right to be supported? But we have never used this right. We would rather put up with anything than be an obstacle to the Good News about Christ.

13 Don't you realize that those who work in the temple get their meals from the offerings brought to the temple? And those who serve at the altar get a share of the sacrificial offerings.

14 In the same way, the Lord ordered that those who preach the Good News should be supported by those who benefit from it.

15 Yet I have never used any of these rights. And I am not writing this to suggest that I want to start now. In fact, I would rather die than lose my right to boast about preaching without charge.

Though Paul made a decision to forgo receiving monetary remuneration from the Corinthians, Scripture supports the idea of ministers being properly paid. Furthermore, experience consistently demonstrates that churches that properly care for their pastors tend to thrive, while those churches which do not tend to provide such care flounder and fail.

In concluding this chapter, let me share with you an example of John Wesley, someone who personified the idea that ministry is work:

John Wesley averaged, during a period of 54 years, about 5,000 miles a year, making in all some 290,000 miles, a distance equal to circumnavigating the globe about twelve times. It must not be forgotten that most of this travel was on horseback. John Wesley preached not less than 15 sermons a week—frequently many more. These sermons were delivered mostly in the open air [outdoors], and under circumstances such as to test the nerve of the most vigorous frame. He did, in the matter of preaching, what no other man ever did. He preached, on average, for a period of 54 years,

15 sermons a week, making in all 42,400, besides numberless exhortations and addresses on a great variety of occasions. While traveling, Wesley read extensively. He read not less than 1,200 volumes, on all subjects. Wesley's literary labors were also immense. It is said that Mr. Wesley's works including abridgments and translations, amounted to some 200 volumes.[55]

I want this passage to inspire you, not intimidate you. So don't feel like you need to do what Wesley did; just know that the same God who empowered him to do what he was called to do will enable you to do what you are called to do. God's not going to give you the grace to fulfill someone else's calling, and it's futile to compete with others or even compare yourself to them.

While our labors and output may not rival Wesley's, let us nonetheless be committed to the tasks that God has placed before us. There is work to be done, a most vital work, and God's servants—those called to the fivefold ministry and other levels of leadership—must lead the way.

---

[55] http://www.goforthall.org/articles/jw_bio.html. From a biographical sketch of John Wesley taken from the following sources: "John Wesley and His Doctrine" by W. MacDonald; *Life of the Rev. John Wesley* by Joseph Benson; and *Life of John Wesley* by John Telford.

Quotes Worth Remembering

"Ministry is spelled W-O-R-K."
—Kenneth W. Hagin

"Ministry is pretty simple. Love people and help them."
—T.L. Osborne

"There are three stages in the work of God: impossible, difficult, done."
—James Hudson Taylor

"Work with all your might, but never trust in your work.
Pray with all your might for the blessing in God, but work at the same time
with all diligence, with all patience, with all perseverance.
Pray, then, and work. Work and pray.
And still again pray, and then work."
—George Muller

Questions for Reflection and Discussion

1. When He was here on earth, Jesus said, "The harvest truly is plentiful, but the laborers are few. Therefore pray the Lord of the harvest to send out laborers into His harvest" (Matthew 9:37–38). How relevant is this particular prayer today? To what degree do you feel that you and your efforts are an answer to that prayer?

2. This chapter states, "Ministry work is not something that we do *for* God. Rather, it is something that we do *with* God." How real is this statement to you? Is it still a philosophical concept, or is it something you have tangibly experienced? Describe ways that you have partnered together with God to accomplish something.

3. We noted that Paul used the analogies of soldier, athlete, and farmer to illustrate the work of the ministry (2 Timothy 2:3–6). What about each of these activities illustrates the various aspects of ministerial work?

4. Paul indicated that Scripture causes the man of God to be "complete, thoroughly equipped for every good work." How does Scripture cause you to be equipped, and in what way are scriptures the actual tools of your trade? How is Second Timothy 3:17 actualized in your life?

5. James Hudson Taylor was quoted as saying, "There are three stages in the work of God: impossible, difficult, done." Why do you think he said that? Can you think of any examples that would illustrate his statement?

REFLECTIONS FROM READERS

Dennis and Jeanne Cook, missionaries to Panama, write:

Having served as missionaries in Panama since 1981, we have had the joy of working for the Lord among the indigenous in the Darien Jungle. Of course we've been heavily engaged in all the expected activities of ministry such as preaching, teaching, praying, and shepherding the people. But our work is far from exclusively spiritual in nature. Over the years, we have had to acquire and employ natural skills in order to be able to participate in spiritual activities.

Leaving the Leper Colony where we enjoyed an apartment and some conveniences, we entered into the Darien Jungle to minister to the Choco Indians. After winning acceptance of the village, we were faced with learning to survive in primitive conditions. We learned how to cook our meals with wood or corn cobs in a hole in the earth. We learned how to climb up logs with steps cut out of them and sleep in primitive grass roof huts without falling off onto the ground (the huts had no walls). We learned to wash our clothes with harsh lye soap on rocks in the river—the same river in which we bathed and went to the bathroom. We learned how to walk in the jungle by stepping on top of logs and then over them instead of just stepping over them and being surprised by a snake on the other side.

When people felt we were trustworthy, we were free to start sharing the Gospel with them. We had to travel by foot or by boat for many hours on end, dealing with heat, rain, mud, and insects just to arrive at a village to share Jesus. On these trips, we carried the old reel-to-reel movie projectors and a generator for light. We did not have microphones, but we used our voices to the extent that often left us voiceless.

One of the secrets of success is to win the right to speak into people's lives. Until they knew our heart and love for them, we got right down in the dirt, mud, or cement with them. We did not demand them to become like North Americans in their worship of God; instead, we assimilated into their culture, allowing them to worship from their hearts. As we sowed, some of the physical labor was taken up by those who had seen the love of Jesus demonstrated in the natural activities of life. And as our support grew, we started building churches with the manpower supplied by us and some of the Indians. When we were able to have Bible schools in the villages, we walked or used horses or canoes, and lugged the books, paper, and whatever else we needed to accomplish the vision God gave.

Melody from Colorado writes:

I am a pastor's wife, a seamstress, an avid reader, a cook, a homeschooling mom, a musician, an organizer, and a problem-solver. Somewhere around the age of thirty—maybe I was a late learner—I learned to really embrace work. And I mean the toilet scrubbing, cabinet cleaning, and doing paperwork kind of work. I know it was the Lord who created this joy in me, because, while I was always responsible, I had really struggled against laziness. I rarely yielded to it, but the desire to be inactive was a constant temptation, especially if I was in the middle of a good book. So I felt sorry for myself when I had work to do, and I felt guilty if I was relaxing, and none of this was very pleasant.

Today I love to work. It is fun for me; and once work becomes fun, it isn't work anymore. I love cooking for folks who are struggling; I love visiting people in the hospital; and I really love going after wayward sheep (Christians who've wandered)—they almost always come home if I go fetch them (again, and again, and again). But I love it. And I do all of this "work" in balance with my family's needs, which is another kind of joyful work that I've readily embraced.

Greg from Florida writes:

I had the opportunity to start my work career when I was about twelve years old. My dad had instilled into me that all people need to work, and that working hard would bring greater things into my life. I started as a shoe shine boy at the local barber shop. I shined people's shoes and also spit-shined the local National Guard soldiers' boots. The more effort I put into shining the boots, the more tips I received. This established my desire to work hard.

Today I own two businesses and pastor a church with a weekly attendance of about two hundred fifty people. Now my work habits are not only shaped by earthly reward, but also— and even more so—by the desire to be the best godly employer

I can possibly be. I get up every day asking God to help me be what He has called me to be and to shape me into a caring employer. God's principles of honesty and fairness now rule my work life, but before I was baptized in the Holy Spirit, I only cared about me and the money. Because I now understand God's desire for me on the job, I am a better employer and person.

A strong work ethic is one result of seeking God first. Working is a vehicle by which God instills important values such as honor, self-worth, and achievement. To follow through and do what I say I will do is a guideline for a successful work ethic. It seems that a lot of people today look for a reason not to go to work. I get up every single day and thank God for the opportunity to work. I learn daily how to put the fruit of the Spirit into operation and allow the Lord to mold my work life.

CHAPTER SEVEN

The Judgment of Our Works: We Will Answer to Jesus

"There is no inconsistency in saying that God rewards good works, provided we understand that nevertheless men obtain eternal life gratuitously."
—John Calvin

Eternal life is a gift. It is given by God through His grace and received by people through faith—that means trusting in Who Jesus is and what He did for us. Having said that, God has also made it abundantly clear that even though we have freely received forgiveness, justification, and acceptance, we will also be rewarded according to our works.

As a young person growing up, I saw some pamphlets that dealt with "judgment day." Somehow, I got the impression that God was eager to parade all of our past sins, mistakes, and failures in front of everyone. He was, I surmised, going to show everyone's—even His own children's—innermost thoughts on some type of big movie screen in heaven. I could not have imagined a more embarrassing and humiliating event.

If you are a believer, that is not what your day of judgment is going to entail. Aren't you grateful and thankful for the fact that our sins have been forgiven through the death, burial, and resurrection of Jesus Christ? We need to understand that the issue of eternal life has already been settled. Thank God for what Jesus said on this subject: "Most assuredly, I say to you, he who hears My word and believes in Him who sent Me has everlasting life, and shall not come into judgment, but has passed from death into life" (John 5:24).

There is, however, another judgment spoken of in Scripture called the Great White Throne Judgment (Revelation 20:11–15). This does not involve the believer but is for those who rejected Christ, for those whose names are not found written in the Lamb's Book of Life. Revelation 20:13 says, "And they were judged, each one according to his works." There are other references to "judgment according to works" that also carry negative connotations:

- ❖ Nehemiah had been opposed by certain enemies, and he prayed, "My God, remember Tobiah and Sanballat, according to these their works, and the prophetess Noadiah and the rest of the prophets who would have made me afraid" (Nehemiah 6:14).

- ❖ Paul spoke of false ministers—agents of Satan—who would be judged according to their works, saying, "Therefore it is no great thing if his ministers also transform themselves into ministers of righteousness, whose end will be according to their works" (2 Corinthians 11:15).

- ❖ Paul also recounted a man who had viciously opposed him, saying, "Alexander the coppersmith did me much harm. May the Lord repay him according to his works" (2 Timothy 4:14).

Every person—saint and sinner—should realize that their conduct on this earth has eternal ramifications and consequences. Though the nature of what believers and unbelievers face is very different, we should be mindful of what we do with our lives—our work on this earth matters.

❖ Paul admonished the Christians in Rome, "But why do you judge your brother? Or why do you show contempt for your brother? For we shall all stand before the judgment seat of Christ," and, "Each of us shall give account of himself to God" (Romans 14:10, 12).

❖ To the Corinthians, Paul wrote, "So whether we are here in this body or away from this body, our goal is to please him. For we must all stand before Christ to be judged. We will each receive whatever we deserve for the good or evil we have done in this earthly body" (2 Corinthians 5:9–10, *NLT*).

❖ In Revelation 14:13, we read, "Then I heard a voice from heaven saying to me, 'Write: "Blessed are the dead who die in the Lord from now on."' 'Yes,' says the Spirit, 'that they may rest from their labors, and their works follow them.'" *The Message* renders the latter part of this verse, "Blessed rest from their hard, hard work. None of what they've done is wasted; God blesses them for it all in the end."

Believers should not dread standing before Jesus; rather, it's an event that we should anticipate with great joy. Imagine all those who have labored in love and served others with their lives being honored and rewarded by Jesus! This can not only give us hope for the future, but can motivate us today.

1 JOHN 4:15–17
15 Whoever confesses that Jesus is the Son of God, God abides in him, and he in God.
16 And we have known and believed the love that God has for us. God is love, and he who abides in love abides in God, and God in him.

17 Love has been perfected among us in this: that we may have boldness in the day of judgment; because as He is, so are we in this world.

It is important to understand how God sees us and how He will interact with us in the future. It is God's nature to not only forgive, but to also reward His children. Some people think that God is aggressively looking for ways and reasons to punish His children. If God wanted to punish us, all He had to do was withhold Jesus.

Eternal Rewards and Crowns in Heaven

God is giving in nature, grateful for our good works and generous to reward us. Consider these Scriptures that deal with the rewarding nature of our Heavenly Father:

❖ In Matthew chapter 6, Jesus speaks of the proper way to give charitable gifts, to pray, and to fast—not for the recognition or the praises of men. He says to do these things discreetly before the Father, "and your Father who sees in secret will Himself reward you openly" (Matthew 6:4, 6, 18).

❖ Matthew 10:42 teaches us that our works don't have to be glamorous or sensational to be appreciated and rewarded by God, saying, "And whoever gives one of these little ones only a cup of cold water in the name of a disciple, assuredly, I say to you, he shall by no means lose his reward."

❖ "For the Son of Man will come in the glory of His Father with His angels, and then He will reward each according to his works" (Matthew 16:27).

❖ Hebrews 6:10–12 (*NLT*) not only reminds us of God's reward-ing nature, but this passage also includes a strong exhortation to continue in good works:

10 For God is not unjust. He will not forget how hard you have worked for him and how you have shown your love to him by caring for other believers, as you still do.

11 Our great desire is that you will keep on loving others as long as life lasts, in order to make certain that what you hope for will come true.

12 Then you will not become spiritually dull and indiffer-ent. Instead, you will follow the example of those who are going to inherit God's promises because of their faith and endurance.

❖ Hebrews 11:6 says, "But without faith it is impossible to please Him, for he who comes to God must believe that He is, and that He is a rewarder of those who diligently seek Him."

❖ When Moses chose obedience to God over the wealth of Egypt, Hebrews 11:26 says that "he was looking ahead to his great reward" (*NLT*). *The Message* version renders this, "He was looking ahead, anticipating the payoff."

❖ "And remember that the heavenly Father to whom you pray has no favorites. He will judge or reward you according to what you do. So you must live in reverent fear of him during your time here as 'temporary residents'" (1 Peter 1:17, *NLT*).

❖ "And behold, I am coming quickly, and My reward is with Me, to give to every one according to his work" (Revelation 22:12).

God's inclination to reward His faithful servants is also seen in the various New Testament references to the crowns that God will bestow.

❖ Paul mentioned "an imperishable crown" that awaits the faithful spiritual athlete (1 Corinthians 9:25).

❖ As Paul reflected on his spiritual journey that is coming to an end, he said, "There is laid up for me the crown of righteousness, which the Lord, the righteous Judge, will give to me on that Day, and not to me only but also to all who have loved His appearing" (2 Timothy 4:8).

❖ Peter told the elders in various churches, "You will receive a crown of never-ending glory and honor" (1 Peter 5:4, *NLT*).

❖ James encouraged believers, "God blesses those who patiently endure testing and temptation. Afterward they will receive the crown of life that God has promised to those who love him" (James 1:12, *NLT*).

❖ To the believers in Smyrna who remained faithful in the face of great persecution, Jesus personally promised "I will give you the crown of life" (Revelation 2:10).

❖ To the church in Philadelphia, Jesus said, "Keep a tight grip on what you have so no one distracts you and steals your crown" (Revelation 3:11, *MSG*).

God is generous and keen to reward those who have labored together with Him. This is not a God who seeks to punish believers, but One who is pleased by our willingness to work with Him and by our grace-inspired efforts for His Kingdom.

However, these gracious rewards are not automatically guaranteed. In fact, if we study all of these verses in context, we see the indication that potential rewards can be lost. This idea is reinforced by Hebrews 10:35–36, which says, "Do not, therefore, fling away your fearless confidence, for it carries a great and glorious compensation of reward. For you have need of steadfast patience and endurance, so that you may perform and fully accomplish the will of God, and thus receive and carry away [and enjoy to the full] what is promised" (*AMP*).

In addition to understanding that perseverance is necessary to receive the crowns that heaven offers, it's also important to recognize the ultimate purpose of these rewards. The purpose of these crowns is not so that believers can strut around heaven like peacocks, boasting of their accomplishments. Rather, we see the purpose of these rewards in the example set by the elders around the throne of God.

REVELATION 4:10–11
10 The twenty-four elders fall down before Him who sits on the throne and worship Him who lives forever and ever, and cast their crowns before the throne, saying:
11 "You are worthy, O Lord, To receive glory and honor and power; For You created all things, And by Your will they exist and were created."

Ultimately, everything in the universe, including the rewards we receive in heaven, are designed for the glory of the Creator. When we work with that understanding and with that intent, we are aligned to work hand-in-hand with God.

The Fire Will Reveal Our Works

One of the things that Paul made clear in his teaching to believers is that it is *our works*, and not us personally, that will be judged at the judgment seat of Christ. Paul also recognized that different people play different roles in the building of the church. He said, "I have laid the foundation, and another builds on it" (1 Corinthians 3:10). Having established that Jesus is the only true foundation, he then said the following:

1 CORINTHIANS 3:12–15 (*NLT*)

12 Anyone who builds on that foundation may use a variety of materials—gold, silver, jewels, wood, hay, or straw.

13 But on the judgment day, fire will reveal what kind of work each builder has done. The fire will show if a person's work has any value.

14 If the work survives, that builder will receive a reward.

15 But if the work is burned up, the builder will suffer great loss. The builder will be saved, but like someone barely escaping through a wall of flames.

I want you to notice the regular recurrence of the word "works." In this passage, Paul is discussing

❖ the kind of work we do,

❖ the value of the work we do,

❖ the endurance (or longevity) of the work we do,

❖ the loss that occurs if the work is burned up, and

❖ the reward that is bestowed if the work survives.

Notice that Paul said that even if the work is burned up, the builder will still be saved, even though it will be "like someone barely escaping through a wall of flames." This judgment is not about whether a believer— a worker—will make it to heaven or not; this is about the type of reward (or lack thereof) that is given for that believer's works.

What Is the Criteria for the Judgment of Our Works?

In school, sometimes a teacher will let the students know ahead of time what type of information will be covered on an upcoming test. That way, students can apply themselves and study specific material in order to do well on that test. Since every believer wants to hear Jesus say, "Well done, good and faithful servant" (Matthew 25:21, 23; Luke 19:17), it is comforting and reassuring to know that God's Word makes clear to us the areas that will be considered at the judgment seat of Christ.

1. Motives

Even as far back as the Old Testament, Scripture reveals that God is concerned about the motives of mens' hearts, not the image they project. When the prophet Samuel was impressed with the kingly appearance of David's oldest brother, Eliab, God corrected him by saying, "Do not look at his appearance or at his physical stature, because I have refused him. For the LORD does not see as man sees; for man looks at the outward appearance, but the LORD looks at the heart" (1 Samuel 16:7). Eliab was rejected, even though he looked the part. Instead, God chose David to be the next king, saying, "I have found David the son of Jesse, a man after My own heart, who will do all My will" (Acts 13:22).

Earlier in this chapter, we learned that people who discreetly work unto the Father will be rewarded (Matthew 6:4, 6, 18). Jesus spoke this truth as a contrast to the hypocrites who endeavored to make a spectacle of themselves in order to be seen by and have the glory of men. Jesus' statement about the latter? The hypocrites "get applause, true, but that's all they get" (Matthew 6:2, *MSG*). In other words, they receive recognition from man, but they'll receive no reward from God.

Of those whose motives were pure, Jesus said, "Your Father who sees in secret will Himself reward you openly" (Matthew 6:4). Note that rewards will be given very visibly. Motives matter! Paul reinforced this whole concept powerfully when he instructed, "So don't make judgments about anyone ahead of time—before the Lord returns. For he will bring our darkest secrets to light and will reveal our private motives. Then God will give to each one whatever praise is due" (1 Corinthians 4:5, *NLT*).

This leads me to believe that we may be very surprised in heaven when we see the rewards believers receive (or don't receive). There may be some who we thought did great things, but if they were motived by pride, greed, or other ungodly motives, they may forfeit the heavenly rewards that could have been theirs. God sees through the smoke and mirrors and false images that people project. If people are more focused on their PR than on producing genuine fruit, they might be in for a big surprise when they stand before Jesus.

There may be others in heaven we never thought much about because their work was primarily behind the scenes; few on earth may have even noticed their labors. They didn't draw attention to themselves, but heaven was keeping track of their efforts and sacrifices. Maybe they were people who prayed, cleaned the building, or drove a bus to transport kids to Sunday school, but they did what they did with pure hearts to honor God and serve people.

One thing is certain: God will not reward people based on the glamor, prestige, or visibility of peoples' positions or titles. God will judge our works based on the motives of our hearts—*why* we did what we did as we carried out our responsibilities in life.

The prevalence of verses about motives throughout Scripture gives us an idea of how important this issue is to God.

❖ "The LORD's light penetrates the human spirit, exposing every hidden motive" (Proverbs 20:27, *NLT*).

❖ "People may be pure in their own eyes, but the LORD examines their motives" (Proverbs 16:2, *NLT*).

❖ "We justify our actions by appearances; God examines our motives" (Proverbs 21:2, *MSG*).

❖ "But I, the LORD, search all hearts and examine secret motives. I give all people their due rewards, according to what their actions deserve" (Jeremiah 17:10, *NLT*).

❖ "For we speak as messengers approved by God to be entrusted with the Good News. Our purpose is to please God, not people. He alone examines the motives of our hearts" (1 Thessalonians 2:4).

❖ After describing the Word of God as being "sharper than any two edged sword," Hebrews 4:12 says that it "is a discerner of the thoughts and intents of the heart" and proceeds to say that "there is no creature hidden from [God's] sight, but all things are naked and open to the eyes of Him to whom we must give account" (Hebrews 4:12–13).

❖ "All the churches shall know that I am He who searches the minds and hearts. And I will give to each one of you according to your works" (Revelation 2:23, *MSG*).

Motives are so paramount that Paul advised everyone—even servants—to keep a good attitude and to maintain good motives:

EPHESIANS 6:5–8

5 Bondservants, be obedient to those who are your masters according to the flesh, with fear and trembling, in sincerity of heart, as to Christ;

6 not with eyeservice, as men-pleasers, but as bondservants of Christ, doing the will of God from the heart,

7 with goodwill doing service, as to the Lord, and not to men,

8 knowing that whatever good anyone does, he will receive the same from the Lord, whether he is a slave or free.

Work for God and His glory? Absolutely. But make sure your motives, intents, and attitudes are godly too.

2. The Royal Law: To Love

One place where love is mentioned in connection with the idea of rewards is in what we call the Sermon on the Mount. Jesus preached, "But love your enemies, do good, and lend, hoping for nothing in return; and your reward will be great, and you will be sons of the Most High" (Luke 6:35). The Apostle James referred to this commandment to love as "the royal law" and gives us very clear instruction regarding how our works on this earth will be evaluated.

JAMES 2:8, 12

8 If you really fulfill the royal law according to the Scripture, "You shall love your neighbor as yourself," you do well;

12 So speak and so do as those who will be judged by the law of liberty.

Of course, love—loving God and loving our neighbor—was the basis for what Jesus said were the two greatest commandments (Matthew 22:36–39), so it should be no surprise that James dignified the exercising of divine love by referring to it as "the royal law" and the "law of liberty."

James taught that the love of God will be the basis for the judgment of everything we say and do. Paul also extolled the lofty and grand nature of love in this timeless treatise:

1 CORINTHIANS 13:1–3

1 Though I speak with the tongues of men and of angels, but have not love, I have become sounding brass or a clanging cymbal.

2 And though I have the gift of prophecy, and understand all mysteries and all knowledge, and though I have all faith, so that I could remove mountains, but have not love, I am nothing.

3 And though I bestow all my goods to feed the poor, and though I give my body to be burned, but have not love, it profits me nothing.

It's okay to anticipate a reward, but we must be motivated by love. If we do good things without being motivated by love, the person we do the work for (or give the gift to) will be benefitted, but we ourselves likely forfeit the eternal reward that would have been ours had we only been operating out of the love of God.

3. Faithfulness

In First Timothy 1:12, Paul says, "And I thank Christ Jesus our Lord who has enabled me, because He counted me faithful, putting me into the ministry." God does not initially call us because we have been faithful; He calls us "according to His own purpose and grace which was given to us in Christ Jesus before time began" (2 Timothy 1:9). However, when God promotes individuals into higher levels of service and responsibilities, it is typically closely related to their having been faithful in their previous duties. In First Corinthians 4:2, Paul writes, "It is [essentially] required of stewards that a man should be found faithful [proving himself worthy of trust]" (*AMP*).

In my book *In Search of Timothy*, I dedicate an entire chapter to the topic of faithfulness—a tremendously important subject. While I am not going to repeat the teaching here, let me share a few thoughts concerning the attributes and characteristics of a faithful person.

A faithful person is all of the following:

- ❖ Active in achieving
- ❖ Committed in covenant
- ❖ Conscientious in commitments
- ❖ Dependable in details
- ❖ Diligent in duties
- ❖ Fervent in functioning
- ❖ Large in loyalty
- ❖ Meticulous in mission
- ❖ Persistent in progressing
- ❖ Proactive in projects
- ❖ Proven in performing
- ❖ Reliable in responsibilities
- ❖ Steadfast in serving
- ❖ Trustworthy in tasks

When you consider these traits and the great results they produce, it's no surprise that Proverbs 28:20 says, "A faithful man will abound with blessings." The *New Living Translation* renders this same verse, "The trustworthy person will get a rich reward."

It makes sense that the rewards of faithfulness can be realized both here on earth and hereafter in heaven. After all, First Timothy 4:8 says,

"Physical training is good, but training for godliness is much better, promising benefits in this life and in the life to come" (*NLT*). Some blessings and rewards might be exclusively received for earth or for heaven, but this verse makes it clear that certain rewards can be realized both "in this life and in the life to come." I believe faithfulness is one of those traits that brings us benefits and rewards in both realms.

Jesus stressed the value and importance of faithfulness in a parable in which He described what a master would say to two servants who had been diligent in administering the resources that had been entrusted to them. To each of the servants the master said, "Well done, you upright (honorable, admirable) and faithful servant! You have been faithful and trustworthy over a little; I will put you in charge of much. Enter into and share the joy (the delight, the blessedness) which your master enjoys" (Matthew 25:21, 23, *AMP*). This parable also reveals the fact that in some cases, one reward of work well done is that we are then privileged to do more work (see Matthew 25:28). Jonas Salk said, "The reward for work well done is the opportunity to do more." When pastors or supervisors look for someone to whom they can give responsibility, they don't look for someone who is inactive and unproductive; they look for someone who has been diligent and productive with the responsibilities he or she already has. As Theodore Roosevelt once stated, "Big jobs usually go to the men who prove their ability to outgrow small ones."

At the end of our earthly journey, the reward for faithfulness will be to hear the Lord Jesus say to each of us, "Well done, good and faithful servant" (Matthew 25:21). During our earthly journey, the reward for faithfulness may be that we receive the privilege of taking on more responsibilities in order to be a greater blessing to others.

4. Potential

Not only does the parable of the talents (Matthew 25:14–30) teach the importance of faithfulness, but we also learn that not everyone has the same inherent potential. In the story, we read that the master "gave five bags of silver to one, two bags of silver to another, and one bag of silver to the last—dividing it in proportion to their abilities" (Matthew 25:15, *NLT*). Jesus does not expect the person with one bag of silver to earn five bags of silver (as the first individual did). Jesus only wants each person to do the best job with what he or she has to work with, according to the potential that each one possesses.

As much as people desire equality and want the world to be fair in every way, it's a simple fact that we don't all have the same potential. This is not an issue of our intrinsic value as human beings, nor is it an issue of superiority or inferiority. It's merely a fact stated by Paul, when he said, "In his grace, God has given us different gifts for doing certain things well" (Romans 12:6, *NLT*).

Even in natural matters, it's not likely that anyone will excel in all areas. In high school, I discovered that I had more of an aptitude toward English and history than I did toward math and science. The first two topics came pretty easy for me, while the latter subjects did not. I may not have the potential to become an astrophysicist, an NBA star, or an opera singer, but I can become what God designed me to be—and that should be my goal. Time spent comparing myself to others is wasted time, and bemoaning not having the gifts others possess will produce nothing but frustration and discouragement. My focus and endeavors must be toward becoming the best *me* that I can be, fulfilling God's assignment for *my* life.

We are not clones; we were uniquely created and are uniquely gifted. We are not all going to have the same abilities and potential. Can you imagine a rabbit watching a bird fly and deciding, *If I just try hard enough, keep a positive attitude, and really believe, someday I'll be able to fly.* The point is not for the rabbit to try to be a bird, but for the rabbit to be and do what he was born to be and do.

We will not be judged based on someone else's potential. God is not going to ask you if your works measured up to the potential that He gave to Billy Graham. We must apply ourselves to using the gifts and abilities God gave to us, and endeavor to fulfill the potential that we possess.

5. Knowledge

We are accountable for what we know, not for what we don't know. Deuteronomy 29:29 says, "The LORD our God has secrets known to no one. We are not accountable for them, but we and our children are accountable forever for all that he has revealed to us, so that we may obey all the terms of these instructions" (*NLT*). A particular parable that Jesus told gives strong indication that God takes into account our knowledge of His will when He evaluates and rewards our works.

LUKE 12:47–48 (*NLT*)

47 And a servant who knows what the master wants, but isn't prepared and doesn't carry out those instructions, will be severely punished.
48 But someone who does not know, and then does something wrong, will be punished only lightly. When someone has been given much, much will be required in return; and when someone has been entrusted with much, even more will be required.

From these words, we understand that the more we know, the more we will be held accountable. Someone might hear that and think, *If knowledge makes me more accountable, I'll just deliberately stay ignorant of God's will, and then I can't be held accountable.* To seek such a loophole is futile. Deliberately remaining ignorant is a form of disobedience upon which heaven certainly does not smile. It seems reasonable that God would hold us accountable for what we know, and for what we could have known had we only applied ourselves.

Other scriptures also support the idea that we are accountable for and will be evaluated based on what we know. The following scriptures deal more with another type of judgment than that of believers' works—they deal with the sin issue. However, the principle of accountability based on knowledge shown in these verses is transcendent, and I believe the principle applies across the board.

- ❖ "Jesus said, 'If you were really blind, you would be blameless, but since you claim to see everything so well, you're accountable for every fault and failure" (John 9:41, *MSG*).

- ❖ "If I had not come and spoken to them, they would have no sin, but now they have no excuse for their sin. . . . If I had not done among them the works which no one else did, they would have no sin; but now they have seen and also hated both Me and My Father" (John 15:22, 24).

- ❖ "God overlooks it as long as you don't know any better—but that time is past. The unknown is now known, and he's calling for a radical life-change" (Acts 17:30, *MSG*).

- ❖ "Therefore, to him who knows to do good and does not do it, to him it is sin" (James 4:17).

What is the appropriate response to these truths? We simply need to walk in the light that we have and do the things that we know we should do. Then, we can joyfully and confidently anticipate great rewards.

6. Obedience

A person could do a lot of things, even good things, and still miss out on a rich reward. The question is not, "Are we doing a lot of good things?" The real question is, "Are we doing the things we are supposed to be doing?" This brings us to the issue of obedience.

Paul clarified, "For this reason also I wrote you: to test you to see if you are obedient in everything" (2 Corinthians 2:9, *NET*). Interestingly, Paul mentioned obedience in the context of being tested, or taking a test. Some people confuse the enemy's temptations with God's testing. When Satan tempts people, it is a solicitation to disobey God, which results in destruction. When God tests people, it is an opportunity to obey Him, which results in blessing.[56] God looks at our obedience, and our obedience to His Word is important to Him.

When Saul was king, he received specific instructions from the Lord through Samuel about what the Israelites were to do following a battle with the Amalekites. Instead of destroying everything as God directly commanded, Saul and the Israelites kept "the best of the sheep, goats, cattle, and plunder to sacrifice to the LORD" (1 Samuel 15:21, *NLT*). Some might think that it was commendable for Saul and his men to honor God with a sacrifice, but God did not want them arbitrarily deciding how to carry out His work; He wanted them to obey His directives.

The prophet, speaking by the word of the Lord, told Saul, "What is more pleasing to the LORD: your burnt offerings and sacrifices or your obedience to his voice? Listen! Obedience is better than sacrifice, and submission is better than offering the fat of rams. Rebellion is as sinful as witchcraft, and stubbornness as bad as worshiping idols. So because you have rejected the command of the LORD, he has rejected you as king"

---

[56]See James 1:13 and also the account of Abraham and Isaac in Genesis chapter 22.

(1 Samuel 15:22–23). God wants us to serve Him, but He wants us to serve Him His way, on His terms. Saul failed the test of obedience, and no doubt lost the reward he could have received.

Speaking of the Israelites who died in the wilderness and failed to receive the fullness of God's blessings, Hebrews 4:11 says, "Thus we must make every effort to enter that rest, so that no one may fall by following the same pattern of disobedience" (*NET*). Obedience is not just an issue of *starting* right, but of also *staying* right. Jesus reminded us, "No one, having put his hand to the plow, and looking back, is fit for the kingdom of God" (Luke 9:62). Part of obedience to God is embracing a task and sticking to it. That doesn't mean that we'll never experience changes or transitions in our assignments, but it means that we aren't quitters or easily discouraged. We keep moving forward, and we continue to do that which is pleasing to God. As Andrew Murray said so well, "Oh, when shall we learn how unspeakably pleasing obedience is in God's sight, and how unspeakable is the reward He bestows upon it."[57]

7. Quality

While wholesome motives are certainly important, we also want to recognize the vital role that quality plays when it comes to rewards. I heard Pastor Scott Wilson say, "If you want to hear God say, 'Well done,' you need to do something well."

God is not a harsh, demanding taskmaster, but He does desire our best. Don't we want people to give their best when we are the recipients of their efforts? If you go to get your car repaired, do you want the mechanic to do a mediocre, slipshod job, or do you want him to give his best effort? If you go for surgery, do you want the doctor to merely have good motives and intentions, or do you want the surgeon to do excellent work?

---

[57] Murray, Andrew. *School of Obedience* (Floyd, VA: Sublime Books, 2014).

It's wonderful when people do their work with love, humility, and a great attitude, but when it comes right down to it, we also want the people helping us to be expertly trained and highly proficient in their work. Should we do any less for God—or for others—when we serve them?

When Paul talked about the works that will survive the fiery examination, he spoke of high quality materials—gold, silver, and jewels. In the same phrase, he implied that the wood, hay, and straw would not survive the test (1 Corinthians 3:12–15). Quality matters!

Even though quality matters and should always be our goal, don't let a fear of failure keep you from trying. If you are paralyzed by a fear of falling short, you'll never receive the practice that is necessary to improve your skills. What's more, if you refuse to do anything until you feel that you can do it perfectly, you'll never even get started. Proficiency really does come from practice, so don't hesitate to serve God and others, no matter how imperfect you consider your efforts. Even if you make mistakes, learn from them, and you'll watch your efforts become more and more fruitful. Let's strive for excellence, but remember that God never beats us down when we fall short of perfection.

Ultimately, we are saved by grace, but we will be rewarded according to our works. God has communicated clear criteria for how He will evaluate what we have done on this earth, and we are wise to apply ourselves to be fruitful and productive for His glory and to do it according to His prescribed ways.

Quotes Worth Remembering

"Show me a man who cannot bother to do little things and I'll show you a man who cannot be trusted to do big things."
—Lawrence D. Bell

"Every act of virtue is an ingredient unto reward."
—Jeremy Taylor

"Whatever you are, be a good one."
—Abraham Lincoln

"Woe to that man who runs when God has not sent him; and woe to him who refuses to run, or who ceases to run, when God has sent him."
—Adam Clarke

"It is not the being seen of men that is wrong, but doing these things for the purpose of being seen of men. The problem with the hypocrite is his motivation. He does not want to be holy; he only wants to seem to be holy. He is more concerned with his reputation for righteousness than about actually becoming righteous. The approbation of men matters more to him than the approval of God."
—Augustine

Questions for Reflection and Discussion

1. How have you perceived the judgment seat of Christ in the past? Have you seen it more as a place of punishment for past sins, or as a place of reward for good works? Has reading this chapter changed your perspective on the judgment seat of Christ, and if so, how has your perspective changed?

2. Conduct a self-evaluation in each of the following areas. Do you need to make any major adjustments?

   A. Motives: Am I keeping my heart right, and am I doing things for the right reasons?

   B. The Royal Law: To Love: Does the love of God dwelling within me influence and govern my attitudes and actions?

   C. Faithfulness: Am I diligent and conscientious? Would others consider me trustworthy, dependable, and reliable?

   D. Potential: Instead of comparing myself to or competing with others, am I doing the best I can with the skills, talents, and abilities that God has given me?

   E. Knowledge: Am I living and serving according to the knowledge I have?

   F. Obedience: Am I doing the things that God has asked me to do?

   G. Quality: Am I accomplishing my tasks to the best of my ability? Is excellence important to me?

3. When you think about standing before the Lord Jesus Christ and presenting an account of your works here on earth, are you filled with a

sense of uneasiness and discomfort, or does the thought evoke positive anticipation and expectation?

4. If there were some adjustments that you could make in your life right now that would result in your receiving a greater reward in heaven, what would those adjustments be?

5. Are you confident that you grasp the distinction between being "saved by grace through faith," and yet being "rewarded according to your works?" Can you define or describe the difference?

CHAPTER EIGHT

The Works We Reject:
Not All Works
Are Good Works

"The supreme end of all education is expert discernment in all things—the power to tell the good from the bad, the genuine from the counterfeit, and to prefer the good and the genuine to the bad and the counterfeit."
—Samuel Johnson

Thus far, we have been extolling the many virtues and benefits of work. We've seen that God is a worker, Jesus is a worker, and we are called to be workers. And yet there are certain types of works that the Bible clearly denounces. Therefore, we need to be both discerning and selective about the types of work we embrace and in which we engage. Paul warned us, "Test all things; hold fast what is good" (1 Thessalonians 5:21). Let's take a look at some of the categories of works that are not to be a part of a believer's life.

1. We Reject Evil Works

Jesus came into the world because of God's love (John 3:16). Jesus didn't come because *we* were good, but because *God* was good. Jesus was life in the midst of death and light in the midst of darkness. While some received Him and accepted the blessing that He brought, others were offended and despised Him deeply. Jesus says of the world, "It hates Me because I testify of it that its works are evil" (John 7:7).

Evil works were nothing new to the generation in which Jesus lived. From the very early days of man, the root of sin and the fruit of wickedness had marred God's plan for His creation. Much has been said about the original transgression involving Adam and Eve, but evil works quickly began to appear in their posterity. In First John 3:12, we are admonished to love one another "not as Cain who was of the wicked one and murdered his brother. And why did he murder him? Because his works were evil and his brother's righteous." Evil works were so predominant and pervasive that First John 3:8 says, "He who sins is of the devil, for the devil has sinned from the beginning. For this purpose the Son of God was manifested, that He might destroy the works of the devil."

Throughout the New Testament, several references educate believers about the nature of Satan's work and the fruit of sin, and admonish believers to shun these things:

- ❖ "The night is far spent, the day is at hand. Therefore let us cast off the works of darkness, and let us put on the armor of light" (Romans 13:12).

- ❖ "Now the works of the flesh are evident, which are: adultery, fornication, uncleanness, lewdness, idolatry, sorcery, hatred, contentions, jealousies, outbursts of wrath, selfish ambitions, dissensions, heresies, envy, murders, drunkenness, revelries, and the like; of which I tell you beforehand, just as I also told you in time past, that those who practice such things will not inherit the kingdom of God " (Galatians 5:19–21).

❖ "And have no fellowship with the unfruitful works of darkness, but rather expose them" (Ephesians 5:11).

❖ "…who, being past feeling, have given themselves over to lewdness, to work all uncleanness with greediness" (Ephesians 4:19).

❖ "And you, who once were alienated and enemies in your mind by wicked works, yet now He has reconciled" (Colossians 1:21).

❖ "The coming of the lawless one is according to the working of Satan, with all power, signs, and lying wonders" (2 Thessalonians 2:9).

❖ "They profess to know God, but in works they deny Him, being abominable, disobedient, and disqualified for every good work" (Titus 1:16).

❖ "But if ye have bitter envying and strife in your hearts, glory not, and lie not against the truth. This wisdom descendeth not from above, but is earthly, sensual, devilish. For where envying and strife is, there is confusion and every evil work" (James 3:14–16, *KJV*).

You will note that we are lumping the works we're to shun into one large category. Even though there can be some variances between the works of the devil, works of darkness, works of the flesh, wicked works, and the working of Satan, they are all works with which we want no association.

2. We Reject Works as a Means of Obtaining Salvation

The list of evil works is pretty obvious. Most people—even people who don't claim to be followers of Jesus—would acknowledge that murder, stealing, lying, and so forth are wrong. We need to understand, though, that seemingly good works can also be problematic if they deceive people into thinking that their so-called good works can somehow put them in right relationship with God. Our works, no matter how sincere we may think we are, simply cannot produce righteousness.

Actually, our engaging in so-called "good works" can lull us into a false sense of security, until we are erroneously thinking that we have somehow earned, deserved, or become worthy of salvation. Doing something good may temporarily ease our conscience or give us a good feeling, but it can never remove underlying sin or impart the gift of righteousness. Only Jesus can do that.

Isaiah articulated an important reality about fallen humanity when he proclaimed that "we are all infected and impure with sin. When we display our righteous deeds, they are nothing but filthy rags" (Isaiah 64:6, *NLT*). Because of this innate condition, man has to have a Savior other than himself; man cannot be his own Savior. Trusting in ourselves or our own efforts for salvation is a complete exercise in futility. Consider the following:

❖ "God saved you by his grace when you believed. And you can't take credit for this; it is a gift from God. Salvation is not a reward for the good things we have done, so none of us can boast about it" (Ephesians 2:8–9, *NLT*). *The Message* version renders these verses, "Saving is all his idea, and all his work. All we do is trust him enough to let him do it. It's God's gift from start to finish! We don't play the major role. If we did, we'd probably go around bragging that we'd done the whole thing!"

❖ In Second Timothy 1:9, Paul speaks of God "who has saved us and called us with a holy calling, not according to our works, but according to His own purpose and grace which was given to us in Christ Jesus before time began."

❖ Paul also taught that God "saved us, not because of the righteous things we had done, but because of his mercy. He washed away our sins, giving us a new birth and new life through the Holy Spirit" (Titus 3:5, *NLT*).

Works serve a definite function in living out and expressing the Christian life, but they are not the way to becoming a Christian. No one can ever be good enough or do enough good deeds or even be religious enough to merit forgiveness and salvation. Becoming a child of God results from receiving as a free gift all that Jesus did for us and putting all of our faith and trust in Him.

If you are reading this right now and realize that you have been trusting in yourself or trusting in your works for salvation, please turn to the back of the book and pray the prayer of salvation that is there, putting all of your trust and confidence in who Jesus is and what He did for you.

Many of the "works" that people have often relied on to earn salvation have to do with attempted compliance regarding the Mosaic Law, the laws of the Old Testament. Galatians 2:16 says, "Knowing that a man is not justified by the works of the law but by faith in Jesus Christ, even we have believed in Christ Jesus, that we might be justified by faith in Christ and not by the works of the law; for by the works of the law no flesh shall be justified." Trying to justify ourselves by adhering to Mosaic Law, or any law, is futile and akin to trying to earn salvation through dead works.

What are dead works? They are any works that are incapable of producing life. Any attempts we may undertake to justify ourselves are useless. Only the work of Christ—His work of love on the cross—is capable of bringing us the life that causes us to be forgiven and delivered from the power of darkness. In Hebrews 6:1, we learn that "repentance from dead works" is one of the elementary principles of the doctrine of Christ. *The*

Amplified Bible says "repentance and abandonment of dead works (dead formalism)," and *The Message* admonishes believers to "[turn their] back on 'salvation by self-help.'"

Simply put, the grace of God expressed toward us in the death, burial, and resurrection of Jesus provides for us a salvation and redemption that we simply could never have merited by our own efforts. Hebrews 9:14 says, "How much more shall the blood of Christ, who through the eternal Spirit offered Himself without spot to God, cleanse your conscience from dead works to serve the living God?" Mature Christians understand that they are saved by the grace of God, and that while their works may express or give evidence to their salvation, those works in no way are the basis for being loved, forgiven, or accepted. It was Christ's work of redemption on the cross that is the basis for our salvation, a gift that is given freely by God and received by faith alone, not earned by our works in any way.

3. We Reject Works Done out of Compulsion

There are individuals who, for one reason or another, have become compulsive in their relationship with work. Far from being lazy, they've swung to the other side of the spectrum and work frantically, always in a state of desperation. Some are driven by a misperception of God, perceiving Him to be more like the harsh taskmasters of Egypt than the Gentle Shepherd of Psalm 23. Let's look at the "Taskmaster Syndrome." In the Book of Exodus, we see the nature of this compulsive work environment described in clear terms:

- ❖ "They appointed brutal slave drivers over them, hoping to wear them down with crushing labor" (Exodus 1:11, *NLT*).

- ❖ "They made their lives bitter, forcing them to mix mortar and make bricks and do all the work in the fields. They were ruthless in all their demands" (Exodus 1:14, *NLT*).

❖ "Pharaoh sent this order to the Egyptian slave drivers and the Israelite foremen: 'Do not supply any more straw for making bricks. Make the people get it themselves! But still require them to make the same number of bricks as before. Don't reduce the quota.... Load them down with more work. Make them sweat!'" (Exodus 5:6–9, *NLT*).

❖ "The Egyptian slave drivers continued to push hard. 'Meet your daily quota of bricks, just as you did when we provided you with straw!' they demanded. Then they whipped the Israelite foremen they had put in charge of the work crews" (Exodus 5:13–14, *NLT*).

These verses remind me of a sign I saw once that said, "The beatings shall continue until morale improves." Of course, the sign was supposed to be humorous, but some people can relate to this kind of work atmosphere.

Even though natural bosses have the potential to be demanding of us, that's not what I'm addressing in this chapter. The "taskmaster" I'm referring to is the misperception that some people have of God. Some people perceive God as One who is impossible to please, who is always demanding more, more, more.

It is understandable that people who perceive God as a harsh taskmaster consistently feel driven and seldom have peace. If you perceive God this way, you may frequently:

❖ feel like you never measure up,

❖ see yourself as inferior,

❖ worry that God is always angry at you,

❖ think that God is always disappointed with you,

❖ be in a constant state of turmoil,

165

❖ feel like no matter what you do it's never enough,

❖ perceive that God demands you meet impossible standards,

❖ go through the motions and mechanics of religious activity, but with no joy,

❖ feel like you are a gerbil in an exercise wheel, and

❖ live in a frantic state, fearful of making a mistake and missing God's will.

If this list describes you, please take time to meditate on Psalm 23. Get to know Jesus as your Great Shepherd! He is not a harsh taskmaster. Remember that the Lord will lead you with a sense of peace; therefore, you can be assured that any sense of panic, drivenness, or compulsion is not from Him.

How do people get under these kinds of bondage? Sometimes unhealthy influences affect people's sincere desire to please God, and these Christians can begin to feel intense pressure that often masquerades as religiosity. While some people may not become involved in the things of God at all, others may become religiously driven. People who suffer under spiritual compulsion live in a pressure-cooker of religious expectations and condemnation. They're continually bombarded with the following types of intrusive, anxious thoughts:

❖ "You're not praying enough."

❖ "You're not studying enough."

❖ "You're not fasting enough."

❖ "You're not witnessing enough."

❖ "You're supposed to be in full-time ministry."

❖ "You're out of the will of God."

❖ "If you were really saved, you'd be more fruitful."

❖ "You're not even called to the ministry."

Satan is still the accuser of the brethren (Revelation 12:10), and as the enemy of our souls, he will try to get us unsettled, upset, and confused. He will attempt to twist essentially good desires or deeds in order to torment Christians with condemnation and bondage because they are "never doing enough." Eventually, the person wears himself out mentally, physically, or emotionally—or all three—because he can never measure up to the constant demand to "do more" or "do better."

Christians who are driven in this way will also often compare themselves with others, feeling bad about themselves because they don't possess all the same gifts that others do. But when we work, we need to work this way:

❖ from a position of being accepted, not in an attempt to earn acceptance;

❖ from a position of possessing salvation, not in an attempt to earn salvation; and

❖ from a position of knowing God's unconditional love, not in an attempt to try to earn God's love.

We need to know that our Father is not a harsh taskmaster—that is a counterfeit perception of God. Isaiah described God this way: "He will feed His flock like a shepherd; He will gather the lambs with His arm, and carry them in His bosom, and gently lead those who are with young" (Isaiah 40:11). Similarly, the Apostle John wrote, "For this is the love of God, that we keep His commandments. And His commandments are not burdensome" (1 John 5:3).

Some of the things God says in His Word—the things He asks us to do—may be challenging to our flesh, but they're refreshing and life-giving to our spirit. Our works—the things we do for God—are to be grace-based, love-motivated, and Spirit-led. When we embrace His assignments, we find fulfillment and joy, not compulsion and condemnation.

4. We Reject Works that Are Tainted by Corruption or Idolatry

The Apostle John ended his first epistle with an admonition for believers to abstain from idolatry. Modern believers might think that idolatry was restricted to cultures that worshipped actual statues of gods and goddesses in temples, but *The Amplified* version of First John 5:21 makes this concept more applicable to us all. It reads, "Little children, keep yourselves from idols (false gods)—[from anything and everything that would occupy the place in your heart due to God, from any sort of substitute for Him that would take first place in your life]."

Christians must be vigilant to keep God and godly values as top priorities, certainly higher than jobs and money. It can be tempting to do otherwise. In the movie *It's a Wonderful Life*, George Bailey (played by Jimmy Stewart) is struggling financially as he endeavors to keep the family-owned business in Bedford Falls afloat. Though he is actively helping others reach their dreams through the Bailey Savings and Loan, he can't help but yearn for greater prosperity, nicer cars, and exotic travel.

In a period of struggle, George Bailey is offered a lucrative position by Mr. Potter, the rich, greedy, conniving, corrupt bank owner. George tells Mr. Potter that he'll talk with his wife about the offer and shakes his hand; in doing so, George suddenly comes to himself. He looks at his hand and wipes it off as though merely shaking hands with Mr. Potter has somehow contaminated him. He realized that to abandon his current work and join up with Potter would be a violation of his own conscience.

A pastor friend of mine once told his congregation, "Some of you have a job that is actually helping the devil do his work on the earth. It's important for people to ask, 'Is my job helping to advance the wrong kingdom?'" My friend said that as he preached along these lines, the Holy Spirit miraculously moved in two people's lives. One was a lady who was the head of the human resources department for a casino. She had been reluctant to take the job, but someone from her church had encouraged her, saying, "It's just a job." Over time, she became more and more uncomfortable as she saw the lives of customers deteriorate before her eyes and cocktail waitresses become prostitutes. She realized that she had a hand in all of this and resigned. In another instance, a medical doctor resigned from a lucrative job that included helping rural medical practitioners conduct safe abortions. She now works for a great orphanage and is starting a program for pregnant teen girls.

Some people will find themselves in situations where they simply cannot, in good conscience, continue to fulfill tasks that they believe are detrimental to their own well-being or that of others. Some Christians might find themselves desiring to work in an entirely Christian setting where their coworkers share their values and moral standards. Certainly, some are called to do just that. However, not every Christian is called to work exclusively among fellow believers.

While some Christians may desire to work in a church or ministry setting, most believers will work in secular settings where some or perhaps all, of their coworkers will not share their biblical values. Should a Christian run away from an environment simply because it is not predominantly Christian? I don't think so. We're not in heaven yet, so we won't find any workplace that's perfect. While I don't recommend working in an environment that destroys our witness, brings unbearable grief, or presents unreasonable levels of temptation, we must keep in mind that we are called to be light and salt in this fallen world.

Talking to God the Father about believers, Jesus said, "I do not pray that You should take them out of the world, but that You should keep them from the evil one" (John 17:15). How can believers influence the world, being the salt and light that Jesus describes in Matthew 5:13–16, if they are totally isolated from unbelievers?[58] Paul told believers to "live clean, innocent lives as children of God, shining like bright lights in a world full of crooked and perverse people" (Philippians 2:15, *NLT*).

Perhaps no one demonstrated this concept better than Daniel. This young Jewish man had been carried away into Babylonian captivity and was selected to be placed into special training to serve in the king's palace. Those selected were educated "in the language and literature of Babylon" (Daniel 1:4, *NLT*). Though Daniel had to work within the Babylonian system, he did not allow that system to hold ascendancy in his heart. Nothing and no one could take the place of His God in the core of his being. In Daniel 1:8, we read, "But Daniel was determined not to defile himself by eating the food and wine given to them by the king. He asked the chief of staff for permission not to eat these unacceptable foods" (*NLT*).

Daniel's determination to keep himself pure did not diminish his effectiveness or productivity in his work. Instead, Daniel excelled "in all matters of wisdom and understanding about which the king examined them, he found them ten times better than all the magicians and astrologers who were in all his realm" (Daniel 1:20, *NLT*). Forced to work around beliefs and practices to which he would have personally objected, Daniel stayed focused on his work, and his efforts eclipsed that of those around

---

[58] See First Corinthians 5:9–10.

him. Twice, Daniel was referred to as having "an excellent spirit" (Daniel 5:12; 6:3).

Daniel, as well as his three friends Shadrach, Meshach, and Abednego, understood that their jobs were not their god. Their boss was not their god, and their paycheck (or whatever compensation or rewards they received) was not their god. Following their example, we can keep ourselves holy and work to create positive, God-honoring results even in unwholesome environments. In James 1:27, we see that "pure and undefiled religion" not only entails caring for widows and orphans, but it also entails:

❖ "refusing to let the world corrupt you" (*NLT*),

❖ "guard[ing] against corruption from the godless world" (*MSG*), and

❖ "keep[ing] oneself unspotted and uncontaminated from the world" (*AMP*).

Let's make sure that our energies and efforts are being spent wisely. Life is too precious, and our time is too important to invest wrongly. Every false way, every counterfeit path, is just a distraction and diversion from the true joy and fulfillment that God has for us as we walk in His ways and fulfill His plans for our lives.

Quotes Worth Remembering

"The greatest enemy to human souls is the self-righteous spirit which makes men look to themselves for salvation."
—Charles H. Spurgeon

"To realize God's presence is the one sovereign remedy against temptation."
—Francois Fenelon

"Holy joy will be oil to the wheels of our obedience."
—Matthew Henry

"There is no greater threat to our devotion to Christ than our service for Christ."
—Oswald Chambers

"Joy, not grit, is the hallmark of holy obedience. We need to be light-hearted in what we do to avoid taking ourselves too seriously. It is a cheerful revolt against self and pride."
—Richard J. Foster

Questions for Reflection and Discussion

1. Have you allowed God to work deeply and thoroughly in your life so that evil works, works of darkness, and works of the flesh are no longer dominating you or being expressed through your life?

2. Are you confident that your salvation is based on faith in Jesus alone and that you are not looking to your own efforts to save you? Have you repented from dead works and ceased from thinking that your compliance to works of the law will somehow cause you to earn God's love or favor?

3. Do you see God as a Good Shepherd who gives you peace, or do you see Him as a harsh taskmaster, One who relentlessly drives you to produce more and more? Have you learned to walk and work in peace, or do you sometimes struggle with a compulsive drive?

4. Are you able to maintain a positive attitude even if you work in a negative environment? How do you stay built up and maintain your integrity in such an atmosphere? Can you relate to Daniel's experience; if so, how?

5. How much of your work is done with joy? Do you remain light-hearted and maintain a good sense of humor? Do you refrain from being too intense and taking yourself too seriously (even though you take your work for God seriously)?

CHAPTER NINE

Works and Rest:
Pacing Ourselves
for the Long-Haul

"Working constantly may be visible proof that deep
inside we do not trust God."[59]
—Bill Bright

Have you ever found yourself stretched to the breaking point, juggling way too many responsibilities and feeling like you'll never get caught up? The Apostle Paul made a reference to a time of restlessness he experienced, and the overall picture he painted is one of distress. In Second Corinthians 7:5, he recounts, "When we came to Macedonia, our bodies had no rest, but we were troubled on every side. Outside were conflicts, inside were fears." Can you relate to such a situation?

Richard Swenson wisely offers, "We must have some room to breathe. We need freedom to think and permission to heal. Our relationships are being starved to death by velocity. No one has time to listen, let alone love.

---

[59] Bright, Bill. *The Joy of Faithful Obedience* (Colorado Springs, Colorado: Cook Communications Ministries, 2005), 61.

Is God pro-exhaustion? Doesn't He lead people by still waters anymore?"[60]
To Dr. Swenson's last question, Jesus answers a resounding "Yes!" The
Savior, who is the same yesterday, today, and forever, says, "Come to Me, all
you who labor and are heavy laden, and I will give you rest. Take My yoke
upon you and learn from Me, for I am gentle and lowly in heart, and you
will find rest for your souls. For My yoke is easy and My burden is light"
(Matthew 11:28–30). *The Message* version renders this passage this way:

> Are you tired? Worn out? Burned out on religion? Come to me.
> Get away with me and you'll recover your life. I'll show you how
> to take a real rest. Walk with me and work with me—watch how
> I do it. Learn the unforced rhythms of grace. I won't lay anything
> heavy or ill-fitting on you. Keep company with me and you'll learn
> to live freely and lightly.

As much as Scripture advocates having a strong work ethic and
working diligently, the Bible also stresses the need and importance of rest.
During the time that Jesus trained His disciples, He made sure that they
understood the importance of taking breaks and resting.

MARK 6:30–32 (*NLT*):

**30 The apostles returned to Jesus from their ministry tour and
told him all they had done and taught.**

**31 Then Jesus said, "Let's go off by ourselves to a quiet place and
rest awhile." He said this because there were so many people
coming and going that Jesus and his apostles didn't even have
time to eat.**

**32 So they left by boat for a quiet place, where they could be
alone.**

---

[60] Swenson, Richard A. M.D. *Margin* (Colorado Springs, CO: NavPress, 1992), 30.

In this particular story, Jesus may be trying to get some rest for His disciples even more than for Himself. The disciples were the ones who had been out traveling and preaching. But Jesus wasn't averse to resting when He was tired. When Jesus was traveling through Samaria, "Jacob's well was there; and Jesus, tired from the long walk, sat wearily beside the well about noontime" (John 4:6 *NLT*). This is common sense, isn't it? Jesus was tired, so He took a break.

Scripture contains many wonderful promises about rest:

❖ God told Moses, "My Presence will go with you, and I will give you rest" (Exodus 33:14).

❖ "I will both lie down in peace, and sleep; For You alone, O LORD, make me dwell in safety" (Psalm 4:8).

❖ "When you lie down, you will not be afraid; Yes, you will lie down and your sleep will be sweet" (Proverbs 3:24).

❖ "For thus says the LORD God, the Holy One of Israel: 'In returning and rest you shall be saved; In quietness and confidence shall be your strength'" (Isaiah 30:15).

❖ Isaiah 32:17–18 says, "And this righteousness will bring peace. Yes, it will bring quietness and confidence forever. My people will live in safety, quietly at home. They will be at rest" (*NLT*).

❖ "Stop at the crossroads and look around. Ask for the old, godly way, and walk in it. Travel its path, and you will find rest for your souls" (Jeremiah 6:16, *NLT*).

Rest is God's idea. He is cognizant of our work and rewards our labor, but He also wants us to rest.

God Established the Pattern

In the opening chapter of this book, the first passage we shared was Genesis 2:2–3, which says, "And on the seventh day God ended His work which He had done, and He rested on the seventh day from all His work which He had done. Then God blessed the seventh day and sanctified it, because in it He rested from all His work which God had created and made." I don't believe that God rested because He was tired and worn out, but, in part, to set a necessary example for us. Matthew Henry eloquently states, "The eternal God, though infinitely happy in the enjoyment of himself, yet took a satisfaction in the work of his own hands. He did not rest, as one weary, but as one well-pleased with the instances of his own goodness and the manifestations of his own glory."[61] Henry continues, "The sabbath of the Lord is truly honourable, and we have reason to honour it—honour it for the sake of its antiquity, its great Author, the sanctification of the first sabbath by the holy God himself, and by our first parents in innocency, in obedience to him."[62] We can follow God's example in work and in rest.

We also pointed out in the first chapter of this book that God's personal ratio of work to rest was six to one; He worked six days and rested on the seventh. God rested. If we are created in His image and His likeness, then rest is something that is necessary and good for us as well.

In the third chapter of this book, we addressed the fact that man was given a job as part of God's original plan. Genesis 2:15 says, "Then the LORD God took the man and put him in the garden of Eden to tend and keep it." The working part of that verse is clear—Adam was put there to "tend and keep" the garden. However, there's another aspect of this verse that may not be as evident. When the Bible says that God "put him" in the

---

[61] Henry, Matthew. *Matthew Henry's Commentary on the Whole Bible: Complete and Unabridged in One Volume* (Peabody: Hendrickson, 1994).
[62] ibid

garden, that doesn't mean He just stuck Adam there. One commentary says the word "'put' in v. 15 translates the causative form of the verb *nûaḥ*, 'rest,' and so could be rendered literally 'caused to rest.'"[63] *The Pulpit Commentary* says that God "literally caused [Adam] to rest in [the garden] as an abode of happiness and peace."[64]

What does this mean? When God created man and placed him in the garden, He not only gave Adam a work assignment, but He also gave him a beautiful place of rest. Work and rest were both a part of God's plan for man. No doubt the fall complicated things for man, but God's original intentions should give us insight into what God really desires for us.

Let's look at the fourth directive of the Ten Commandments, which gives instructions regarding the Sabbath rest:

EXODUS 20:8–11

8 Remember the Sabbath day, to keep it holy.

9 Six days you shall labor and do all your work,

10 but the seventh day is the Sabbath of the LORD your God. In it you shall do no work: you, nor your son, nor your daughter, nor your male servant, nor your female servant, nor your cattle, nor your stranger who is within your gates.

11 For in six days the LORD made the heavens and the earth, the sea, and all that is in them, and rested the seventh day. Therefore the LORD blessed the Sabbath day and hallowed it.

This was God's Word to the Jewish people, to those who were under the Old Covenant, and it was intended to provide blessing to the people. But by the time of Jesus' ministry, hundreds upon hundreds of man-made traditions had been added to the biblical directives, resulting in a culture

---

[63] Mathews, K. A. *Genesis 1-11:26, The New American Commentary* (Nashville: Broadman & Holman Publishers, 1996), 208.

[64] Spence-Jones, H. D. M. ed. *The Pulpit Commentary*, Genesis (London; New York: Funk & Wagnalls Company, 1909), 46.

steeped in legalism. Some feverishly searched for loopholes to the God-given law so that they could still appear righteous while circumventing the law itself. Noted scholar William Barclay cites an example of this when he comments on Luke 11:46: "One of the forbidden works on the Sabbath was the tying of knots, sailors' or camel drivers' knots and knots in ropes. But a woman might tie the knot in her girdle. Therefore, if a bucket of water had to be raised from a well, a rope could not be knotted to it, but a woman's girdle could, and it could be raised with that!"[65] In this way, the people could say that they were obeying the law, but they had effectively found a way around it. This is part of what legalism does—it focuses on the letter of the law instead of the spirit of the law.

Jesus Clarifies the Purpose of the Sabbath

Jesus had stern words for those who took godly principles that had been originally designed to help people and twisted them into unbearable burdens. In Luke 11:46, Jesus said, "What sorrow also awaits you experts in religious law! For you crush people with unbearable religious demands, and you never lift a finger to ease the burden" (*NLT*). Instead of compassionately trying to help people, the religious leaders just kept piling more requirements on them.

One of the Pharisees' favorite attacks against Jesus pertained to the multitude of legal points that had arisen surrounding the Sabbath. On one occasion, the Pharisees challenged Jesus because the disciples plucked off some grain and ate it as they walked through a field on the Sabbath, which the Pharisees considered a violation of their religious law. Jesus' response to them? "The Sabbath was made to meet the needs of people, and not people to meet the requirements of the Sabbath. So the Son of Man is Lord,

---

[65] Barclay, William, editor. *The Daily Study Bible Series: The Gospel of Luke* (Philadelphia, PA: The Westminster John Knox Press, 1975).

even over the Sabbath!" (Mark 3:27–28, *NLT*). The original intention of honoring the Sabbath saw people abstaining from a regular work day, but the Pharisees had so convoluted the original command that the extreme applications had become an unbearable burden on the people.

The legalistic attitude that Jesus faced continued to be an issue as the church in Jerusalem developed. When certain people tried to make circumcision a requirement for salvation, Peter boldly responded, "Why do you test God by putting a yoke on the neck of the disciples which neither our fathers nor we were able to bear? But we believe that through the grace of the Lord Jesus Christ we shall be saved in the same manner as they" (Acts 15:10–11).

It is vital that we realize that God doesn't ask us to rest so that He can love or accept us. Rather, because He loves us and seeks our welfare, He invites us to rest so that we can live life as He intended us to live it.

While I don't believe we are under the law of the Sabbath, I believe there is a principle of Sabbath that remains. One of the psalms beautifully describes God's desire for us to avoid overwork, especially when driven by anxiety, and to enjoy the rest that is part of God's plan for us.

PSALM 127:1–2

1 Unless the LORD builds the house, they labor in vain who build it; Unless the LORD guards the city, the watchman stays awake in vain.
2 It is vain for you to rise up early, to sit up late, to eat the bread of sorrows; For so He gives His beloved sleep.

The Message renders verse two as saying, "It's useless to rise early and go to bed late, and work your worried fingers to the bone. Don't you know he enjoys giving rest to those he loves?"

Finding the Pace for our Race

It's not that we don't work or that we don't work diligently, but we want to make sure that we work wisely and that we pace ourselves appropriately. Rest is part of God's plan for our lives. We understand the need for rest when we acknowledge that we are finite and not omnipotent. Dave Williams wisely says, "Working too long without a break is a form of pride."[66] Gerald Brooks says, "God's pace always leads to God's peace."

When we really trust God, we believe that God can bless our labors and multiply what is produced; we also believe that God can work above and beyond our efforts, even while we rest. Leonard Sweet and Frank Viola phrase it this way, "God did His most magnificent work while Adam was asleep. This episode contains an important insight: When man rests, God works."[67]

Epaphroditus, one of the Apostle Paul's young associate ministers, almost killed himself because he worked too hard and lacked proper rest. The Philippian church had sent Epaphroditus to help Paul, and help him he did. However, he tried to do too much too fast and brought injury to himself in the process. Speaking of the hard-working Epaphroditus, Paul said, "For the work of Christ he came close to death, not regarding his life, to supply what was lacking in your service toward me" (Philippians 2:30). Wuest renders this same verse, "Because on account of the work of Christ he drew near to death, having recklessly exposed his life in order that he might supply that which was lacking in your sacred service to me."

As workers, we need to know our limits. As employers, we need not test the limits of our employees. As a leader, Jacob knew not to drive those under his care to the point of exhaustion. When he felt Esau pressuring

---

[66] Williams, Dave. *Emerging Leaders* (Lansing, MI, Decapolis Publishing, 2005), 115.
[67] Sweet, Leonard and Frank Viola. *Jesus: A Theography* (Nashville, TN: Thomas Nelson, 2012), 31.

him to keep pace with him, Jacob responded, "You can see, my lord, that some of the children are very young, and the flocks and herds have their young, too. If they are driven too hard, even for one day, all the animals could die. Please, my lord, go ahead of your servant. We will follow slowly, at a pace that is comfortable for the livestock and the children" (Genesis 33:13–14, *NLT*).

Charles Spurgeon, known as the Prince of Preachers, said much about the need for rest in a chapter titled "The Minister's Fainting Fits." Spurgeon faced bouts of depression throughout his ministry, and he felt that rest was a factor in overcoming and preventing such periods of despondency. He explains:

> The bow cannot be always bent without fear of breaking. Repose is as needful to the mind as sleep to the body. . . . Even the earth must lie fallow and have her Sabbaths, and so must we. . . . The Master knows better than to exhaust His servants and quench the light of Israel. Rest time is not waste time. It is economy to gather fresh strength. . . . A little pause prepares the mind for greater service in the good cause. . . . Who can help being out of breath when the race is continued without intermission. . . . It is wisdom to take occasional furlough. In the long run, we shall do more by sometimes doing less. . . . We must every now and then cry halt, and serve the Lord by holy inaction and consecrated leisure.[68]

Even if the Lord were only interested in our labor, He is wise enough to know that we do more work and better work when we're rested and strong. But the Lord is not just interested in what we can do for Him. He offers us rest because He cares about us.

---

[68] Spurgeon, Charles H. *Lectures To My Students* (Grand Rapids, Michigan: Zondervan, 1954), 160–161.

While it's commendable to work hard, it's necessary to pace ourselves and rest properly. Ira Chaleff writes:

> We must do our jobs, not become our jobs. A follower may feel heroic working fifteen-hour days or ninety-hour weeks. Sometimes we feel pressured into long hours by the example the leader is setting. Occasionally, we do need to work this hard for short periods of time. But if excessive time at work becomes a long-standing pattern, we must change it before it depletes our energy and wreaks havoc in other parts of our lives. If we do not assume responsibility for getting the nurturing we need as human beings, we will burn out sooner or later. To serve well, we must be passionately committed to our jobs, but not consumed by that passion.[69]

Some people pride themselves on how much and how hard they work. But a "workaholic" pace cannot be sustained indefinitely. It's better to rest by choice now than to be forced to rest later.

What Does God Offer His People?

Some of the old-time preachers were known to say, "I'd rather burn out than rust out." Wisdom teaches us that we don't have to do either. The Bible reveals the many delights that God offers His people:

❖ Rest: "Rest in the LORD, and wait patiently for Him" (Psalm 37:7).

❖ Refuge: "Oh, the joys of those who take refuge in him!" (Psalm 34:8, *NLT*).

---

[69] Chaleff, Ira. *The Courageous Follower* (San Francisco: Berrett-Koehler Publishers, Inc., 1995). Reprinted with permission of the publisher.

❖ Retreat: "You're my place of quiet retreat; I wait for your Word to renew me" (Psalm 119:114, *MSG*).

❖ Respite: "On Mount Zion—there's respite there! a safe and holy place!" (Obadiah 1:17, *MSG*).

❖ Recovery: "Are you tired? Worn out? Burned out on religion? Come to me. Get away with me and you'll recover your life. I'll show you how to take a real rest" (Matthew 11:28, *MSG*).

❖ Reviving: "I dwell in the high and holy place, with him who has a contrite and humble spirit, to revive the spirit of the humble, and to revive the heart of the contrite ones" (Isaiah 57:15).

❖ Restoration: "He makes me to lie down in green pastures; He leads me beside the still waters. He restores my soul" (Psalm 23:2-3).

❖ Renewal: "But those who wait on the LORD shall renew their strength; They shall mount up with wings like eagles, they shall run and not be weary, they shall walk and not faint" (Isaiah 40:31).

❖ Rejuvenation: "These words hold me up in bad times; yes, your promises rejuvenate me" (Psalm 119:50, *MSG*).

❖ Refreshing: "But I'm in the very presence of God—oh, how refreshing it is!" (Psalm 73:28, *MSG*).

❖ Reflection: "Be still, and know that I am God" (Psalm 46:1). "I will study your commandments and reflect on your ways" (Psalm 119:15, *NLT*). "I reflect at night on who you are, O LORD" (Psalm 119:55, *NLT*).

❖ Relaxation: "I said to myself, 'Relax and rest. God has showered you with blessings'" (Psalm 116:7, *MSG*).

Does God intend for us to work for Him? Absolutely. Does He want us to be effective and productive here on this earth? Certainly. But God also understands our limitations and needs. There is enough time for us to do what God asks of us and still take time to rest and enjoy life. While it's good to have high aspirations, and it's great to be diligent in achieving our goals, it's still important to stop and smell the roses along the way. Paul told Timothy that God "gives us richly all things to enjoy" (1 Timothy 6:17).

The real key to working and enduring is balance—allocating our time and energy properly so that our lives reflect a healthy rhythm. Saint Augustine said it well: "No man has a right to lead such a life of contemplation as to forget in his own ease the service due to his neighbor; nor has any man a right to be so immersed in active life as to the neglect the contemplation of God."

To the weary, the fatigued, the exhausted, and the burnt-out, God has rest for you. God has restoration for you. God has a refreshing for you. We will accomplish far more for God, even if we appear to work less, when we are adequately rested. Let's come to terms with the fact that we are not omnipotent and find the pleasure of a reasonable pace.

Quotes Worth Remembering

"You will break the bow if you always keep it bent."
—Ancient Greek saying

"He that can take rest is greater than he that can take cities."
—Benjamin Franklin

"The stops of a good man are ordained by the Lord as well as his steps."
—George Mueller

"It is our best work that God wants, not the dregs of our exhaustion. I think he must prefer quality to quantity."

—George Macdonald

"Rest in the Lord; wait patiently for Him. In Hebrew, 'Be silent in God, and let Him mould thee.' Keep still, and He will mould thee to the right shape."
—Martin Luther

Questions for Reflection and Discussion

1. Do you see adequate rest as part of God's overall plan for your life, or do you feel guilty when you take time to take care for yourself and rest?

2. Read Matthew 11:28–30 again, both in the *New King James Version* and in *The Message* version. Is this description consistent with the way you perceive Jesus?

3. When it comes to the principle of the Sabbath, do you think you A) tend to disregard it, B) tend to be too legalistic about it, or C) have a habit of honoring and practicing it?

4. Re-read the two paragraphs about Epaphroditus in this chapter and read the full context of Paul's statements about him in Philippians 2:25–30. What lessons can we learn from Epaphroditus' experience?

5. Review the list of "What God Offers His People." Evaluate how you think you're doing in each of the specific areas listed—Rest, Refuge, Retreat, and so forth.

REFLECTIONS FROM READERS

Dan from Nebraska writes:

God will direct us at a very early age. I was given a book called *My First Book of Electricity* when I was 10 years old, and God used that book, which I still have today, to set in motion the course for starting my own company. I love my work because I know that God has called me to do it, and every day I come to work in faith believing for miracles, signs, and wonders to take place with employees, vendors, and customers. Every challenge is met with God by my side. I have declared so many of God's promises, and we see the fulfillment of them on a regular basis. Just to have the opportunity to pray for a customer brings a thrill to my heart.

I started a company in the basement of my house in 1980, then dedicated it—and my life—to the Lord six months later. I began working every waking moment of my life, including weekends, putting every penny away and living on my wife's salary as a helper in a hospital. I can remember the Sunday that I was standing outside, freezing, waiting for a customer to show up at the construction site, and saying to the Lord, "Let this be my last Sunday I have to work." And so it was. I learned that God hears and answers my prayers.

About a year later, my wife encouraged me to stop working on Saturdays since we had a baby by then, and I needed to be more of a father to my child. To this day, I can see myself putting the key into the security system to turn it on as I left that Saturday, saying, "Lord, let this be my last Saturday that I have to work." And so it was. I learned that by trusting God, I could actually work only five days a week and still be profitable.

The principle of working only five days a week might defy a lot of business people's beliefs, but when we commit our life and business to the Lord with true sincerity, a supernatural empowerment or endowment occurs, and God is given the legal right to work in that business. I can testify of wonderful results too numerous to write.

God has called me to be involved in a "marketplace ministry" that provides goods and services while also sharing the Gospel of Jesus Christ and helping businessmen grow in their faith. Believers can be encouraged as they work for their company with excellence, knowing that they are serving Christ and that they will give an account to the Lord when they stand before Him.

EPILOGUE

A Christian Worker's Creed: Charting Our Course for the Future

"At the Day of Judgment, we shall not be asked what we have read, but what we have done."

—Thomas a Kempis

Congratulations. The fact that you finished this book says a lot about you. It tells me that you're deeply interested in the significance of what you do in this life—you care about your works. Perhaps what you've read has simply reinforced and strengthened your beliefs, or maybe it has changed your mindset on some issues. Perhaps it has challenged you about your attitude or encouraged you concerning your work. Above all, I pray that what you have read influences, from the inside out, the way you work and the way you serve. It's what we do with what we know, after all, that really matters.

The enduring actions we take in life, those that stand the test of time, are those that are based upon quality decisions and unwavering commitments.

This kind of resolve occurs when we have a clear picture and understanding of the kind of future we want for ourselves.

With that in mind, I want to summarize many of the scriptural principles that have been presented in this book. I'm doing so in the form of a creed—a document that expresses what has hopefully become your aspiration and guiding beliefs. This is an affirmation, a confession, and a declaration of accepting God's purpose and standard for your life.

§ § § § § §

God, my Creator and Father, is a Worker. Having been created in His image and His likeness, I, too, am a worker. I am called to be an imitator of God and to be a laborer together with Him in the earth.[70]

Jesus Christ, my Lord and Savior, is also a Worker. I proclaim with Jesus that "my Father is always working, and so am I." Like Jesus, I declare, "I must work the works of Him who sent Me," and, "My food is to do the will of Him who sent Me, and to finish His work."[71]

I purpose to let my light shine before men so that they may see my good works and glorify my Father in heaven. I believe the works that Jesus did, I will do also, and greater works, because Jesus has gone to the Father. I have received the empowerment of the Holy Spirit to do His works, and like Jesus I say, "My Father who lives in me does His work through me."[72]

My work on this earth—all that I set my hand to do—is dignified and honorable because I do it all as unto the Lord. All that I do, I do for the glory of God and the benefit of others.[73]

---

[70] Genesis 1:26; Ephesians 5:1–2; 1 Corinthians 3:9
[71] John 5:17; 9:4; 4:34
[72] Matthew 5:16; John 14:12; Acts 1:8; John 14:10, NLT
[73] Colossians 3:17; Romans 15:1–2

Concerning my influence toward others, I determine to follow Moses' example. I will endeavor to show others "the way in which they must walk and the work they must do."[74]

I pray that it will be said of my generation and those in my company, that we accomplished great things because we had a mind to work.[75]

Like Ezra, I pray that I can inspire and influence others—that both my life and my words can say, "Be strong, all you people, and work; for the Lord is with you."[76]

Like Paul, I pray that I am a constant example of someone who helps those in need by working hard. It is my prayer that people who are not Christians will respect the way I live. And if someone asks about my Christian hope, I will always be ready to explain it.[77]

I resolve to embody and personify the traits of industry, diligence, and hard work. I believe that as I excel in my work, I shall stand before kings and not stand before unknown men. Embracing the wisdom of Scripture, I pledge that whatever my hand finds to do, I will do it with all my might.[78]

As an employee, I will respect the instructions of my employers and not just do the minimum that will get me by. I will do my best and work from my heart. I will be ever mindful that Christ is the ultimate Master I am serving and that promotion comes from the Lord.[79]

As an employer, I will not be abusive or threatening, but I will treat my employees considerately, justly, and with fairness, remembering that I also have a "Master"—God in heaven.[80]

---

[74] Exodus 18:20
[75] Nehemiah 4:6
[76] Ezra 2:4
[77] Acts 20:34–35, NLT; 1 Thessalonians 4:11–12, NLT; 1 Peter 3:14–15, NLT
[78] Proverbs 22:29; Ecclesiastes 9:10
[79] Colossians 3:22–24, MSG; Psalm 75:6–7, KJV
[80] Ephesians 6:9, MSG; Colossians 4:1, MSG

I determine to be steadfast, immovable, and always abounding in the work of the Lord. I know that my labor in the Lord is not in vain. I also believe that God makes all grace abound toward me, enabling me to have sufficiency in all things and have an abundance for every good work.[81]

I believe that I am God's workmanship, created in Christ Jesus for good works, which God prepared beforehand for me to walk in them. God, who began a good work in me, will continue His work until it is finally finished on the day when Christ Jesus returns. God is working in me, giving me the desire and the power to do what pleases Him.[82]

With God's help, I will work out my own salvation with fear and trembling; I will be fruitful in every good work and rich in good works. God gives me the power to accomplish all the good things that my faith prompts me to do, and He establishes me in every good work, making me complete in every good work to do His will.[83]

God is not unjust to forget my work and labor of love that I have shown toward His name, in that I have ministered to the saints, and do minister.[84]

I resolve to express a pattern of good works, be zealous for good works, be ready for every good work, and maintain good works.[85]

I will be a doer of the work and will be blessed in what I do. I will show by good conduct that my works are done in the meekness of wisdom. My conduct will be honorable among all people and as they observe my good works, they will glorify God. I will show the truth by my actions.[86]

---

[81] 1 Corinthians 15:58; 2 Corinthians 9:8
[82] Ephesians 2:10; Philippians 1:6, NLT; 2:13, NLT
[83] Philippians 2:12; Colossians 1:10; 1 Timothy 6:18, NLT; 2 Thessalonians 1:11, NLT; 2 Thessalonians 2:16–17; Hebrews 13:21
[84] Hebrews 6:10
[85] Titus 2:7; 2:14; 3:1; 3:8
[86] James 1:25; 3:13; 1 Peter 2:12; 1 John 3:18–19, NLT

As I follow Jesus, He makes me a fisher of men and a laborer in the harvest. The Lord works with me, and I am a laborer together with God.[87]

I have been crucified with Christ, nevertheless I live; yet not I, but Christ lives in me. It is by God's grace that I am what I am, and His grace toward me is not in vain; I labor abundantly, yet not I, but it is the grace of God which is with me.[88]

Like Paul, I labor, striving with all the superhuman energy that God so mightily enkindles and works within me. It is not by my might or by my power, but it is by His Spirit.[89]

Though I labor, I also have rest and renewal in the Lord. Jesus is gentle and lowly in heart. He gives rest to my soul. His yoke is easy, and His burden is light. His righteousness brings me peace; it brings quietness and confidence forever. His Presence goes with me, and He gives me rest.[90]

I have been saved by grace, and yet I will be rewarded according to my works. As I draw my last breaths in this mortal body, I pray that, like Jesus, I will be able to say to God, "I have glorified You on the earth. I have finished the work which You have given Me to do." When I leave this earth, my works will follow me. I shall stand before the judgment seat of Christ, and I will give account of myself to God. Like Moses, I look ahead to a great reward, and I believe there is laid up for me an imperishable crown of righteousness—the crown of life.[91]

ভ ভ ভ ভ ভ

Do these statements resonate with you? Maybe there is something on the inside of you that says, *I may not perfectly measure up to all of these*

---

[87] Matthew 4:19; 9:37–38; Mark 16:20; 1 Corinthians 3:9, KJV
[88] Galatians 2:20; 1 Corinthians 15:10
[89] Colossians 1:29, AMP; Zechariah 4:6
[90] Mathew 11:28–30; Isaiah 32:17–18; Exodus 33:14
[91] Ephesians 2:8–9; Revelation 22:12; John 17:4; Revelation 14:13; Romans 14:10; Hebrews 11:26; 1 Corinthians 9:25; 2 Timothy 4:8; James 1:12, NLT

standards at this moment, but I believe that God is working in me to help build me into that very person. I encourage you to make these declarations a point of reference and a basis of meditation in your life. Let God build these specific beliefs and attributes into your life, and then allow the Holy Spirit to form these traits in your life as you act upon God's Word. May it be said of our generation that we did great things for God, or, more accurately, that God did great things through us, because we had a mind to work.

Appendix

Frequently Asked Questions (and Answers)

Question: In addition to serving God through my regular work and activities, I'd like to begin serving God in a more focused and specific way. How do I begin "working for God"?

Answer: Here are seven questions each of us can ask ourselves to help us begin serving God and working more effectively for Him.

1. What is my level of spiritual consecration?

Are you 100% sold-out to Jesus? Are you willing to sacrifice your comfort and convenience for someone else's benefit? Is there anything you're not willing to do for Jesus? Is there anything that you feel would be beneath you? In days gone by, it was not uncommon to hear people at the altar praying and dedicating their lives to God. A common, heartfelt prayer was, "God, I'll go where You want me to go. I'll do what You want me to do. I'll say what You want me to say." Serving becomes easier when you've totally and completely surrendered all of your heart and life to God. Consecration was clearly modeled for us in the Garden of Gethsemane when Jesus prayed, "Not My will, but Yours, be done" (Luke 22:42, *NKJV*).

2. What is my attitude toward serving?

Many will say they want to be like Jesus, but have they really considered what being like Him entails? Jesus communicated plainly what it means to have "a kingdom attitude." Matthew 20:26–28 says, "Whoever desires to become great among you, let him be your servant. And whoever desires to be first among you, let him be your slave—just as the Son of Man did not come to be served, but to serve, and to give His life a ransom for many." Dr. Martin Luther King Jr. said, "Everybody can be great, because everybody can serve. You don't have to have a college degree to serve. You don't have to make your subject and your verb agree to serve. You only need a heart full of grace, a soul generated by love."

3. What is my level of availability?

A person can have all the *ability* in the world, but it will avail nothing if he or she does not have *availability*. I understand that people are busy, but have we become so busy that we have no time to serve God? We speak of giving God the first portion of our income, and that is good, but wouldn't it be outstanding if all of God's people gave Him a good portion of their time as well? Make it a priority to order your life in such a way that you can give God ample time in worship and in work. Make "seek first the kingdom of God" (Matthew 6:33) a reality in your priorities and in the way you schedule your life.

4. Am I willing to work?

As I've endeavored to communicate throughout this book, "work" is not an unspiritual word. Serving God isn't simply sitting around, having warm, fuzzy feelings and thinking about holy things. God calls us to work. Paul said, "I labor [unto weariness], striving with all the superhuman energy which He so mightily enkindles and works within me" (Colossians 1:29, *AMP*). Jesus said, "Let your light so shine before men, that they may see your good works and glorify your Father in heaven" (Matthew 5:16). People will never see our good works unless we actually work!

5. What do I do well?

God has given each of us certain skills, aptitudes, and gifts. It's not this book's purpose to attempt to delineate between natural abilities and spiritual gifts, but let me simply propose that we use whatever abilities and resources we have for the glory of God and for the betterment of others. A pastor told me about a man who came to him, wanting to preach in his church. The pastor had never met this man and didn't know him at all. While he did not need help in the pulpit (nor would he have entrusted the pulpit to someone he did not know), the pastor discovered that this man was also an electrician and let him know that they had a major project underway and that the church needed a skilled electrician. Fortunately, the man was gracious enough to lend his natural skills to the church, and he did an excellent job serving the church through that avenue. God can use your natural skills for His glory.

6. What are the needs and opportunities around me?

Some Christians struggle because they don't feel like they have a specific leading or a direct word from God regarding what they're supposed to do. Others feel that if they are to do something significant for God, it must be something that is far away and spectacular. John Burroughs said, "The lure of the distant and the difficult is deceptive. The great opportunity is where you are." If you don't know what to do, find someone who is doing something for God and simply begin to help them. Ask your pastor or someone at your church what you can do to serve. Specific direction may come later, but you're being helpful and productive in the meantime. Jesus said, "If you have not been faithful in what is another man's, who will give you what is your own?" (Luke 16:12). In short, bloom where you're planted.

7. Am I willing to take initiative?

Arthur Ashe said, "Start where you are. Use what you have. Do what you can." Be a person who is eager to help others. Don't wait for someone to ask you to serve; proactively look for and embrace the things that need to be done. Albert Hubert said, "Parties who want milk should not seat themselves on a stool in the middle of the field and hope that the cow will back up to them." Don't be afraid to start with small things. If you see a piece of trash on the ground that needs to be picked up, pick it up.

Lean into action, not away from it. Embrace responsibility; don't shun it. Act, and believe that God will bless the work of your hands. If there is something more specialized or more targeted that God wants you to do, He will certainly lead you to it and open the appropriate doors in due time.

🌀🌀🌀🌀🌀

Question: I have a really difficult boss (or difficult coworkers). Should I look for a new job, or stay where I am? If I choose to stay, do you have any advice?

Answer: This is an issue that countless people face. Not only do people have bosses who are challenging to work for, but people often deal with unpleasant coworkers as well. If we approach this from a different perspective, we recognize that there are also some good bosses who have frustrations with difficult employees. The bottom line is that we live in a fallen world and, as Max Lucado once said, we should "lower [our] expectations of earth. This isn't heaven, so don't expect it to be."

Generally speaking, we who live in a free society have the right to step away from an undesirable job and seek employment elsewhere. Having said that, let me mention a couple of other considerations.

First, stepping away from a problematic employment situation does not guarantee that your next place of employment will be free of problems. If you are a person who is prone to run at the first sign of difficulty, you may find that in getting a new job, you are simply jumping out of the frying pan into the fire.

To avoid making a rash decision, I suggest you take Jesus' advice and "count the cost" (Luke 14:28) before you make a major move. Try to avoid impulsive, knee-jerk reactions, and first consider if there are things that you can do to improve your current work situation (which isn't always possible) or if there are ways you can grow spiritually and strengthen yourself in order to improve your resilience and endurance.

If a change is necessary, increase the likelihood of a positive transition by being a continual learner. Always seek to diversify your skills, be well-trained, and invest in yourself to make sure that you have a lot to offer prospective employers. Sometimes, transition means choosing to be self-employed and starting your own business. Whatever you do, you want to cover your decisions in prayer, receive godly and wise counsel, and do all that you can to improve yourself, your knowledge, and your skills.

For those who face challenges at their current place of work but don't necessarily feel inclined to resign and do something different, there is some pretty significant biblical counsel on how to thrive in less-than-ideal environments. Many New Testament believers were slaves, as this was a common practice in the ancient world. While I don't advocate slavery in any way, here is what Peter told people who could not, at that moment, change their situation: "Servants, be submissive to your masters with all fear, not only to the good and gentle, but also to the harsh" (1 Peter 2:18). Peter understood that some of these individuals were in circumstances that were very difficult, and he encouraged them to do what was honorable, to maintain their Christian character, and to exemplify godly traits.

Paul also weighed in on this, encouraging Christian slaves and exhorting Christian masters to do right by one another.

EPHESIANS 6:5–9

5 Slaves, obey your earthly masters with deep respect and fear. Serve them sincerely as you would serve Christ.
6 Try to please them all the time, not just when they are watching you. As slaves of Christ, do the will of God with all your heart.

7 Work with enthusiasm, as though you were working for the Lord rather than for people.

8 Remember that the Lord will reward each one of us for the good we do, whether we are slaves or free.

9 Masters, treat your slaves in the same way. Don't threaten them; remember, you both have the same Master in heaven, and he has no favorites.

Knowing that slaves were able to obtain their freedom under certain circumstances, Paul said to the Christian slaves in Corinth, "Are you a slave? Don't let that worry you—but if you get a chance to be free, take it" (1 Corinthians 7:21, *NLT*). *The New Bible Commentary* says, "Household slaves, except those in the Imperial household, were eligible for release after seven years."[92]

Another commentary remarks, "While Paul valued freedom (and here encouraged slaves to obtain freedom if they had opportunity), he knew any attempt by slaves to abolish slavery would mean certain death. The Romans were ruthless at suppressing slave revolts like the uprising led by Spartacus in 73 B.C."[93] Even in a culture that was highly repressive, Paul encouraged individuals who could gain their freedom—who could advance—to do so. Those who could not gain their freedom, though, were to remain Christ-like in all that they did. Paul admonished, "Slaves must always obey their masters and do their best to please them. They must not talk back or steal, but must show themselves to be entirely trustworthy and good. Then they will make the teaching about God our Savior attractive in every way" (Titus 2:9–10, *NLT*).

---

[92] Carson, D. A., R. T. France, J. A. Motyer and G. J. Wenham, editors. *New Bible Commentary: 21st Century Edition. 4th ed.* (Leicester, England; Downers Grove, IL: Inter-Varsity Press, 1994).

[93] Cabal, Ted, Chad Owen Brand, E. Ray Clendenen, Paul Copan, J.P. Moreland and Doug Powell. *The Apologetics Study Bible: Real Questions, Straight Answers, Stronger Faith* (Nashville, TN: Holman Bible Publishers, 2007).

While it's certainly not wrong to leave a bad workplace and transition into new employment, there are times when God will help us survive and even thrive in less-than-ideal environments, with less-than-ideal coworkers, and with a less-than-ideal boss. Consider Joseph, sold into slavery by his own brothers. He had no way to "apply for a new job" or change his status, but Joseph made the best of the situation in which he found himself.

GENESIS 39:2–4
2 The LORD was with Joseph, and he was a successful man; and he was in the house of his master the Egyptian.
3 And his master saw that the LORD was with him and that the LORD made all he did to prosper in his hand.
4 So Joseph found favor in his sight, and served him.

Joseph's story strongly challenged me when I had a tendency to complain about things that I did not like work-wise. If anyone had a reason to complain, it was Joseph. Instead, he worked hard, he honored the Lord, and the Lord prospered him.

Daniel, a slave during the Babylonian captivity, is another phenomenal example of someone who found a way to thrive in a difficult environment. Rather than bemoan his situation, wallowing in self-pity and losing hope, Daniel excelled in spite of the idolatry that was all around him. Daniel 1:9 says, "Now God had brought Daniel into the favor and goodwill of the chief of the eunuchs." And Daniel 1:20 says, "And in all matters of wisdom and understanding about which the king examined them, he found them ten times better than all the magicians and astrologers who were in all his realm."

I know a Christian who worked for the owner of a large company, and this owner had an explosive temper and foul mouth. Was working in that environment pleasant for my friend all the time? Certainly not. But this gentleman carried himself with godly character and dignity, and over time he won the respect of his boss. At times, his boss would start to explode or begin to cuss, and then he would see this gentleman. Just the presence of this believer would apparently bring conviction upon the owner of the company, because he would restrain himself, calm down, and shut down his own verbal tirade. Sometimes he would even apologize to this believer. I don't know if the company owner ever gave his life to Jesus, but this employee had a profound influence in his life.

Each person has to decide for himself or herself what course of action to take—to stay or to go elsewhere. There's a right way to stay, and there's a right way to go. Whatever you do, use wisdom and trust God to guide your steps.

֍ ֍ ֍ ֍ ֍ ֍

Question: What should employees do when they are asked to do something immoral, unethical, or illegal—or something that would violate their own conscience?

Answer: Some women faced this exact dilemma around the time of the birth of Moses. The king of Egypt had ordered the midwives to murder any Israelite boys who were born. Here's what the Bible says of these brave women: "But because the midwives feared God, they refused to obey the king's orders. They allowed the boys to live, too" (Exodus 1:17, *NLT*).

Individuals who resolve to do what is right and refuse to do what is wrong need to recognize the inherent risk in their courageous decision. In the situation with the Egyptian midwives, though, we see that the blessing God bestowed upon them was rich and rewarding: "So God was good to the midwives, . . . And because the midwives feared God, he gave them families of their own" (Exodus 1:20–21, *NLT*).

Shadrach, Meshach, and Abednego, when they were government officials in Babylon, refused King Nebuchadnezzar's edict to bow down before the golden statue. Faced with the death penalty, they remained respectful toward the king but refused to violate God's commandment. The story of their deliverance is one of the great faith lessons in the Bible (see Daniel 3:1–30).

Joseph also refused to compromise his integrity. In his case, Joseph did not face an ungodly order from his master Potiphar; instead, he endured—and refused—an ungodly sexual advance from his boss' wife. Joseph righteously responded to her, "There is no one greater in this house than I, nor has [Potiphar] kept back anything from me but you, because you are his wife. How then can I do this great wickedness, and sin against God?" (Genesis 39:9). Scorned, Potiphar's wife falsely accused Joseph, and he spent years in prison as a result. God later vindicated Joseph and promoted him highly, but he still suffered as a result of his righteous stand. Believers today who find themselves experiencing problems because of their stand for integrity can take courage from what Peter wrote centuries ago: "For God is pleased with you when you do what you know is right and patiently endure unfair treatment. Of course, you get no credit for being patient if you are beaten for doing wrong. But if you suffer for doing good and endure it patiently, God is pleased with you" (1 Peter 2:19–20, *NLT*).

Under the ministry of John the Baptist, people were powerfully convicted of their need to repent from sin. John did not exhort people to leave their secular professions and enter into some kind of religious work. Instead, he admonished them to conduct themselves righteously while they remained in their existing professions. Even corrupt tax collectors came to be baptized and asked, "Teacher, what should we do?" John replied, "Collect no more taxes than the government requires." Soldiers asked him, "What should we do?" And John replied, "Don't extort money or make false accusations. And be content with your pay" (Luke 3:12–14, *NLT*). We learn from this that believers are called to live and work righteously and honestly. John the Baptist did not ask these individuals to leave their careers, but simply to operate and conduct themselves with integrity.

ᔕ ᔕ ᔕ ᔕ ᔕ ᔕ

Question: What thoughts do you have about retirement and preparing for retirement?

Answer: Of retirement, D. Elton Trueblood said, "For the Christian, retirement is really liberation for service. The retired person may start a wholly new chapter rather than do nothing. The Christian philosophy of work is one which never ends."[94] Personally, I don't want to write a lot about retirement, because I've never been retired. However, I believe it's very important to learn from those who have traveled the road ahead of us. So I asked a great friend who retired from pastoring several years ago to share how he prepared himself for that transition and how he's managing life during retirement. I believe his advice can greatly benefit people and help them to plan and prepare wisely.

From 1980–1983, I was an assistant pastor to Dr. Dan Beller at Evangelistic Temple in Tulsa, Oklahoma. Pastor Beller resigned in 2001 after 34 years of service, but he has continued to serve vibrantly since his official retirement. I asked him to explain some of the preparations he made before retiring; while his remarks are specifically targeted toward pastors (at my request), I believe some of the principles can apply to everyone. I suggest to all readers, pastors included, to seek out the wisdom of a trusted wealth advisor for further suggestions on how to fiscally prepare for retirement.

---

[94] Henry, Carl F.H. editor *Baker's Dictionary of Christian Ethics* (Grand Rapids, Michigan: Baker Book House, 1973), 715.

Dr. Beller writes:

For a pastor, the word "retirement" is a misnomer because we never really retire from doing some kind of ministry; which is to say, we should always be serving others. However, there are definite adjustments that must be made from "full time ministry" to "retirement ministry." Your personal ministry continues in various ways. There will always be someone to whom you can minister and be a witness. Also, your personal study must continue, because the educational process is a lifetime experience. And there will probably still be occasions when you will be invited to speak at churches and participate in weddings, funerals, and other events.

In Proverbs 6:6–8, we are exhorted to be wise like the ant because it gathers food during the harvest (your productive years) and stores up the food for the difficult times after the harvest (your retirement years). As a retired pastor, I can say from experience that it is vital to save resources and be prepared for the retirement years. Some of the areas of preparation include the following:

Prepare Yourself Spiritually

Most of us identify too much with *what we do* instead of *who we are*. This is why some pastors lack a good self-image in retirement. It is therefore important to develop new areas of interest for the retirement years. I recommend several pursuits:

- ❖ Continue to study the Bible and relevant materials. Never stop learning.

- ❖ Continue your prayer life. The first objective in prayer is to maintain your close relationship with God, not to get help for your ministry.

❖ Pray for the active pastors and assist them whenever possible.

❖ Continue to minister in public and private whenever there is a need.

❖ Continue formal studies through the programs of your church association/fellowship, online, or at a local college or university.

Prepare Yourself Financially

Zig Ziglar stated, "Money is not the most important thing in life, but it is reasonably close to oxygen on the 'gotta have it' scale." Inadequate retirement income can lead to a lower lifestyle and disappointment. Social security income is meant to be a supplement to your retirement income and is inadequate as full support. I recommend the following course of action:

❖ Be faithful in giving the Lord's tithes all of your life. Tithing is a prerequisite to financial blessings.

❖ While you are still pastoring, request that your local church appropriate a housing allowance so that you can own your own home by retirement. Also, seek to set up an expense account for church-related car expenses, travel, meals, and so forth.

❖ If your church association/fellowship has a group retirement plan (like a 403(b) or tax sheltered annuity), ask your church to consider making regular contributions on your behalf.

❖ Make annual contributions to a tax-deferred IRA; there are a few types to choose from. A trusted, qualified financial advisor can assist you in finding the instrument that is best for you.

❖ Pay off all debts before retirement. You can save thousands of dollars in interest on the mortgage of your home by making extra principal payments each month. The principal payments, especially at the beginning of a home loan, are usually surprisingly low because much of the payment is interest. Avoid credit card debt because the interest is extremely high; if you do have credit card debt, pay it off first.

❖ It is imperative to start saving for retirement early in life, so do not spend all of your earnings during the productive years. A wealthy man told me his philosophy: "You can have it now, or you can have it later."

❖ There are many practical ways to save and make some of your income available for retirement savings: save by shopping for quality items at a reduced price, by shopping online, or by being aware of sales and rebates at local stores. Save by not eating out as much; expensive coffees add up. Save by using a credit card that gives rebates and has no annual fee.

Prepare Yourself Emotionally

The 24/7 schedule of a pastor or the intense workload of a secular job often prevents having time for leisure and other interests. Without these interests, a person can feel idle and unproductive in retirement. It is therefore important to develop a variety of interests such as hobbies, sports, recreational reading, concerts, and so forth.

A healthy self-image is maintained by realizing who you are in Christ instead of judging yourself by what you do. It is good to remember that we are saved by grace, through faith, and not by works (Ephesians 2:8–9). Yet, we were created to work, and it's important to feel that you are retiring *to* something instead of *from* something. One great way to find purposeful work during retirement is to volunteer at a local church, hospital, or community organization.

When you retire, there will need to be adjustments in your home and marriage. Discuss with your spouse what you mutually want or do not want to experience in retirement. Your spouse has been accustomed to your being gone so much during the work day that your being home more than usual can cause friction. Solutions may include spending time in an office at home or at a local church, volunteering your service outside the home, or golfing or other hobbies with friends. Conversely, it is important to be of help to your spouse to make up for the lack of time that was given when your work schedule was so busy. Spending some private time together or going out to dinner occasionally may be a welcome blessing. If you enjoy traveling, plan and set aside money to take trips together.

Prepare Yourself Physically

Retirement does not mean that you sit down and become inactive, so you must maintain your mental and physical health. Remain active with regular physical exercise: join a local health club, golf, walk in your neighborhood or on a treadmill in your home, and so forth. Consider maintaining a healthy diet with vitamins and supplements. Keep your mind and thoughts healthy and positive.

Prepare Your Successor

In addition to providing quality ministry during your active years of pastoring, one of the most important things you can do before retiring is to help secure the long-term success of the church by preparing your successor and helping raise up a strong ministry team that can work together in leading the church when you step away.

Even though I had a long tenure as pastor (34 years), I was always mindful that someday someone other than me would be filling the role of senior pastor. I felt it was my responsibility to do everything I could to help train the one who would be the future leader of the church. While my long-term associate eventually did take my place, it was with the consensus of the church board and the congregation as well.

The years a pastor spends in retirement often equal half (or more) of the years spent in active ministry. It is important, therefore, to realize that retirement is a very significant era in your life. If you make proper preparation and maintain a positive attitude, retirement can be quite fulfilling and enjoyable.

PRAYER OF SALVATION

God loves you—no matter who you are, no matter what your past. God loves you so much that He gave His one and only begotten Son for you. The Bible tells us that "...whoever believes in Him shall not perish but have eternal life" (John 3:16 NIV). Jesus laid down His life and rose again so that we could spend eternity with Him in heaven and experience His absolute best on earth. If you would like to receive Jesus into your life, say the following prayer out loud and mean it from your heart.

Heavenly Father, I come to You admitting that I am a sinner. Right now, I choose to turn away from sin, and I ask You to cleanse me of all unrighteousness. I believe that Your Son, Jesus, died on the cross to take away my sins. I also believe that He rose again from the dead so that I might be forgiven of my sins and made righteous through faith in Him. I call upon the name of Jesus Christ to be the Savior and Lord of my life. Jesus, I choose to follow You and ask that You fill me with the power of the Holy Spirit. I declare that right now I am a child of God. I am free from sin and full of the right-eousness of God. I am saved in Jesus' name. Amen.

If you prayed this prayer to receive Jesus Christ as your Savior for the first time, please contact us on the Web at **www.harrisonhouse.com** to receive a free book.

Or you may write to us at

Harrison House • P.O. Box 35035 • Tulsa, Oklahoma 74153

The Harrison House Vision

Proclaiming the truth and the power

Of the Gospel of Jesus Christ

With excellence;

Challenging Christians to

Live victoriously,

Grow spiritually,

Know God intimately.

Additional Teaching Resources by Tony Cooke

Available at www.tonycooke.org

Your Place on God's Dream Team: The Making of Champions - Book and Video Series

Through the Storms: Help from Heaven When All Hell Breaks Loose - Book and Video Series

Qualified: Serving God with Integrity and Finishing Your Course with Honor - Book

Grace: The DNA of God - Book and Video Series

In Search of Timothy: Discovering and Developing Greatness in Church Staff and Volunteers - Book, Video Series, Workbook

Life After Death: Rediscovering Life After the Loss of a Loved One - Book

Sign up to receive Tony Cooke's free monthly teaching articles at www.tonycooke.org